Bubbles
& Balloons

Bubbles & Balloons

35 amazing science experiments

Susan Akass

CICO **Kidz**

Published in 2018 by CICO Books
An imprint of Ryland Peters & Small Ltd
20–21 Jockey's Fields, London WC1R 4BW
341 E 116th St, New York, NY 10029

www.rylandpeters.com

10 9 8 7 6 5 4 3 2 1

A CIP catalog record for this book is
available from the Library of Congress
and the British Library.

ISBN: 978 1 78249 577 2

Printed in China

Editor: Katie Hardwicke
Design concept: Eoghan O'Brien
Designer: Alison Fenton
Photographer: Terry Benson
Illustrator: Rachel Boulton

In-house editor: Dawn Bates
In-house designer: Eliana Holder
Art director: Sally Powell
Production manager: Gordana Simakovic
Publishing manager: Penny Craig
Publisher: Cindy Richards

Contents

• •

Introduction 6
Setting Up Your Science Lab 7
Science Investigations 9
A Little Bit About Molecules 12

CHAPTER 1
Brilliant Bubbles

Bubble Wands in all Shapes and Sizes 16
Bubble Mixes 18
The Science of Bubbles 20
Big Wands for Big Bubbles 22
Bubble Colors 26
Floating Bubbles 29
Square Bubbles 31
Bubbles Inside Bubbles 34
Bubble Tennis 36
Bubble Prints 38

CHAPTER 2
Bubbling Brews and Fizzing Foams

Glowing Lava Lamp 42
Pop-up Glove 46
Rainbow Snake 49
Elephant's Toothpaste 52
Shaving Foam Marbling 55
Bobbing Raisins 58
Soda Geyser 60
Fizzing Rocks 62
Bubbling Pondweed 64
Amazing Bubble Wrap 67

CHAPTER 3
Cooking with Bubbles

Whip that Cream 72
Honeycomb Toffee 74
Animal Bread Rolls 78
Bubbling Breakfast Pancakes 82
Erupting Pans 85
Light-as-air Meringues 88
Baked Alaska 92

CHAPTER 4
Balloon Magic

What's that Wailing? 98
How NOT to Pop a Balloon! 100
Skewer a Balloon 102
Balloon Rocket 104
Electric Balloon 107
Black and White Balloons 110
Balloon Fire Extinguisher 112
Hovering Helium 116
How Your Lungs Work 118
Weighing Air 122

Explore Further 126
Index 127
Acknowledgment and Picture Credits 128

Introduction

Everyone smiles when bubbles fill the air or balloons are brought out for parties and celebrations. But bubbles and balloons are also a great place to start having some fun with science. This isn't school science. There are no right and wrong answers, just plenty of different experiments to do that will make you say, "Wow!" and "Awesome!" or "Why does that happen?"

Chapter 1, "Brilliant Bubbles," is all about soap bubbles: how to make a bubble mix, how to make bubble wands from all sorts of different bits and pieces, and how to make some truly extraordinary bubbles ranging from super-sized to square ones.

Bubbles can also include the tiny bubbles that make up foams and these are fascinating too. In **Chapter 2, "Bubbling Brews and Fizzing Foams,"** there are some real WOW experiments where foams explode out of bottles, as well as quieter investigations, where bubbles show you that something unexpected is going on.

Chapter 3, "Cooking with Bubbles," is all based on what you can create in the kitchen. As you will discover, bubbles are an essential part of many delicious recipes, and cooking and science go hand in hand.

Finally, **Chapter 4, "Balloon Magic,"** is about experimenting and discovering with balloons. Balloons, like bubbles, are full of gas but, because they are so much stronger, there is a lot of cool science you can do with them, from making rockets to skewering them without popping them, and using balloons to understand how your lungs work.

Before you start any of the experiments, it is worth building up a stock of some of the basic ingredients and equipment for your Bubbles and Balloons Science Lab—see the lists on pages 7 and 8 to get you started. Each experiment also lists the specific items you will need.

Most items can be found around your home, but there are a few things that you'll need to buy in order to stay safe (and look the part of a scientist!). The first things you need to get hold of are two pairs of safety goggles—one for you and one for any friend or family member who helps you with the experiments. These will protect your eyes and must be worn when you are asked to do so. Take note of the safety advice on page 8 and any safety instructions within the experiments, particularly in the cooking chapter. For some experiments you will need an adult to help you.

Trying out the activities will be great fun, but if you want to find out why something happens, read "Inside the Science" for a scientific explanation for each experiment. There are also suggestions to investigate further in "Let's Investigate." Follow up some of these ideas and you will be well on the way to becoming a true scientist!

Setting Up Your Science Lab

Each experiment in the book includes a list of the ingredients or chemicals, materials, and other equipment you will need. Most of the materials can be found in the kitchen cabinet, but for some experiments you may have to buy or find something special, either from a drug store (pharmacy) or online.

We've listed below the items that you will need regularly, and which will be useful to have in your science lab. Some of the materials are things that you can reuse, perhaps from the recycling bin, or everyday things found around your home. Look out for them (ask before you take!) and build up your collection. When you're cooking, you may need to buy special ingredients, but you should have the equipment already in your kitchen.

Safety equipment
• Two pairs of safety goggles

Chemicals: scientific ingredients

• Acrylic paint

• Baking powder

• Baking soda (bicarbonate of soda)

• Corn starch (cornflour)

• Dish soap (washing-up liquid): In the US, use Joy or Dawn; in the UK and Europe, use Fairy Liquid, Dreft, and Yes.

• Distilled water (hard water areas only)

• Dried yeast

• Food coloring

• Glycerin

• Shaving foam (budget brands are best)

• Sugar

• Sugar-free soda

• Vinegar

Other materials

- Balloon pump (optional but easier than blowing up balloons yourself)
- Balloons (including some long ones and some black and white ones)
- Bamboo skewers
- Bubble wrap
- Chenille stems (pipe cleaners)
- Cotton twine or string
- Dowel
- Drinking straws
- Elastic bands
- Fishing line or kite string
- Funnel
- Garden wire or wire coat hangers
- Hex nuts and bolts
- Paper clips
- Plastic bottles (all sizes)
- Plastic pipettes
- Plastic wrap (clingfilm)
- Screw eyes
- Soda can
- Strong paper or card stock
- Strong sticky tape
- Thumb tacks (drawing pins)
- Yarn

Equipment

- Baking sheets
- Flashlight
- Kettle
- Magnifying glass
- Measuring spoons
- Pots and pans
- Plastic pitchers (jugs)
- Rotary hand whisk or electric beater
- Timer
- Wide bowls or trays

 = STAY SAFE

Science can be dangerous. Chemicals can react together in unexpected ways and cause explosions or splash into your eyes or onto your skin. If you use heat or fire, you can burn yourself. That's why scientists take safety very seriously.

The experiments in this book are not dangerous, but you should still learn to keep yourself safe. Where there is any risk that you could hurt yourself, the book tells you to ask an adult to help (look for the safety symbol shown above). Make sure that you do, especially in the cooking chapter when there is a risk of burns. Also, wear safety goggles when told to—especially when popping balloons—then you will both protect your eyes and really look like a scientist!

Science Investigations

Each of the experiments in this book shows you how to do something that gives exciting results and then tells you what happened, using simple science.

That may be enough for you, but real scientists don't just follow instructions. They ask questions and then try to find out the answers for themselves. So, if you want to be a real scientist, do some more investigating, either by following the suggestions in "Let's Investigate," or by thinking of your own questions. A good question may lead you to carrying out a proper scientific fair test. To do this you will need to:
a) Ask a scientific question.
b) Make a prediction—what do you think will happen and why?
c) Carry out a fair test and make accurate and repeated measurements.

d) Record (write down) your results.
e) Reach a conclusion (decide if your results match your prediction or show something else).

Let's take the bobbing raisin experiment on page 58 as an example, where we discover that raisins in soda bob to the surface and then sink again. The science tells you why it happens, but what makes the raisins bob more or less?

1

First list all the things you could change in the experiment (these are called variables), which might change how the raisins bob. These would be:
- *Size of glass*
- *Type of soda*
- *Level of soda in the glass*
- *Temperature of the soda*
- *Fizziness of the soda (how long the top has been off the soda bottle)*
- *Size of the raisins*

2

Now choose one of these variables to investigate by asking a scientific question that you can test. For that you need to think, "What can I measure or count?" Well, you could count how many times a raisin bobs to the surface in one minute, so your question could be:
Do the smaller raisins bob to the surface more often than the bigger raisins?

3

A good scientist then predicts the answer, with a reason. You might say: *"I think big raisins will bob less often because they need more bubbles around them to lift them to the surface because they are heavier."*

4

Next, plan your test. To make it a fair test you can only change the variable you are investigating: The size of the raisin. The other variables (the glass, the soda, the level, the temperature, and the fizziness) must stay exactly the same.

So your plan would be:

a) I will do the test three times—once with currants (which are like small raisins), once with ordinary raisins, and once with jumbo raisins, keeping all the other variables the same.

b) I will use a minute timer and count the number of times each raisin bobs to the surface of a glass of soda in one minute.

c) I will make a tally chart and mark it each time a raisin comes to the surface.

You will need more than one of each type of raisin because not all raisins behave in exactly the same way. One jumbo raisin might bob a lot of times and another not so many. Three of each kind would be a good number to use—with more it would be hard to count the bobs.

Imagine if you didn't keep the other variables the same. Say, for example, you counted raisins in cold soda and jumbo raisins in warm soda—how would you know if it was the temperature of the soda or the size of the raisins that made a difference?

5

Draw a tally chart to record your results. Carry out your plan and mark down the number of bobs on the chart. See below for an example of some results (not real ones).

Size of raisin	Number of bobs		
	Raisin 1	Raisin 2	Raisin 3
Small (currants)	11111	1111	1111
Medium (raisins)	111	11111	1111111
Big (jumbo raisins)	1111	111111	111111

6

What did you find out? As you have counted more than one raisin in each test you have ended up with lots of numbers. Now you need to do some math to work out the mean (average) number of bobs for each size of raisin.

The mean (average) is what you get when you add up all the bobs for one size of raisin and share it out between the raisins —you can use a calculator for this!

Size of raisin	Number of bobs	Mean
Small (currants)	5+4+4 = 13	13÷3 = **4.33**
Medium (raisins)	3+5+7 = 15	15÷3 = **5**
Big (jumbo raisins)	4+6+6 =16	16÷3 = **5.33**

7

Now look for a pattern. In this example, the jumbo raisins bobbed more than the raisins which bobbed more than the currants. This means that you could write an ER sentence of your results: "The biggER the raisin, the more times it bobbed" or "The smallER the raisin, the fewER times it bobbed," which says the same thing.

Remember your results may not tell you anything. You may have to do the test more times to find a pattern or there may not be a pattern to find. Science is complicated!

8

Finally, *think*. Did your results fit your prediction? If they did, your reasoning may be correct. If they didn't, and they didn't in this example, can you think of a way of explaining what went on? Maybe the bigger raisins had more places for bubbles to form on. It doesn't matter if you are right or wrong. The important thing is to begin thinking scientifically and to have fun doing proper scientific investigations!

A Little Bit About Molecules

Throughout this book you will find the word "molecule" used a lot, so here's a little bit about what it means.

Molecules are what most things are made of, including you! They are unbelievably tiny, but they are not the tiniest things scientists have discovered. Molecules are made of atoms, and even atoms are made of smaller parts, including electrons—another word you'll find in this book.

Think about what you have just read. The sentences are made of words, which are made of letters. If everything in the world is like a written language, the atoms are the letters. There are 26 letters in the Latin alphabet (used here), which can be put together into words in billions of different ways. There are about 100 different types of atoms, so they can be put together in even more ways than letters. The different atoms are called elements.

You may know the names of many elements already: Oxygen, hydrogen, aluminum, iron, gold, silver, copper, chlorine, helium, and carbon are a few of them. These atoms can join up with other atoms to make molecules, just as letters join up to make up words.

Molecules are written down in a code, with letters standing for the atoms. For example:

Water is H_2O = 2 hydrogen (H) atoms + 1 oxygen (O) atom

Carbon dioxide is CO_2 = 1 carbon (C) atom + 2 oxygen (O) atoms

Baking soda (bicarbonate of soda) is $NaHCO_3$ = 1 sodium (Na) atom + 1 hydrogen (H) atom + 1 carbon (C) atom + 3 oxygen (O) atoms

Glucose is $C_6H_{12}O_6$ = 6 carbon (C) atoms + 12 hydrogen (H) atoms + 6 oxygen (O) atoms

Sometimes the code letters (symbols) used for atoms are not obvious; for example, sodium's symbol is Na because it comes from a Latin word natrium. You can find all the names of the elements and their symbols in a special chart called the Periodic Table, which is the starting point for all chemistry. Scientists make models of molecules using different colored balls as atoms, (although atoms don't really look like this). These models help you to understand how the molecules join together in different ways. Look at the diagrams below: The model for water is relatively simple, but glucose is more complex.

Water molecule H_2O

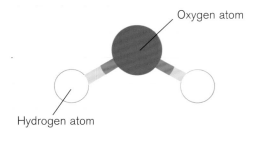

Oxygen atom

Hydrogen atom

Glucose $C_6H_{12}O_6$

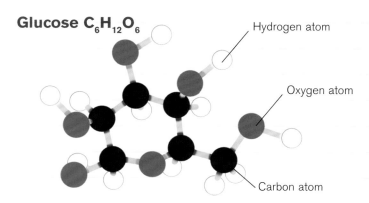

Hydrogen atom

Oxygen atom

Carbon atom

When molecules rearrange themselves or swap atoms with other different molecules to make new substances, it is called a chemical reaction. Sometimes you know chemical reactions are happening because you see bubbles. This is because a gas has been made in the reaction. To create a chemical reaction that produces a gas, try these experiments: Pop-up Glove (see page 46), Elephant's Toothpaste (see page 52), Fizzing Rocks (see page 62), and Honeycomb Toffee (see page 74).

Molecules come in many different shapes and sizes and have different properties, depending on how their atoms are arranged. These different properties help to explain why bubbles behave as they do; to investigate this further, try the following experiments: Square Bubbles (see page 31), Bubble Prints (see page 38), and Shaving Foam Marbling (see page 55). Because balloons are stretchy, they are really helpful to use for scientific investigations into different qualities of molecules, such as weighing gases (see pages 117 and 121), how electrons behave (see page 108), and how color and light are connected (see page 111).

To understand why molecules join together and how they behave, you will have to learn more about electrons and that is getting a bit too complicated for this book! If you are interested, track down some more advanced science books and websites.

FASCINATING FACT

Scientists have found out that atoms can join together in different ways, so we can't say that everything is made of molecules. Some metal atoms, for instance, join together in a lattice or framework, which is not a molecule. The biggest molecule known has over 400,000 atoms.

Chapter 1
Brilliant Bubbles

• •

This chapter shows you how to become an expert bubble blower! Discover the best bubble mixes and make your own bubble wands, from a simple paper cone to a professional tri-string wand for giant bubbles. There are lots of experiments to try that will explain how bubbles work, why they pop, and how you can change their shapes, make art, and play games with just some water, dish soap, and a puff of air!

Bubble Wands in all Shapes and Sizes 16

Bubble Mixes 18

The Science of Bubbles 20

Big Wands for Big Bubbles 22

Bubble Colors 26

Floating Bubbles 29

Square Bubbles 31

Bubbles Inside Bubbles 34

Bubble Tennis 36

Bubble Prints 38

Bubble Wands in all Shapes and Sizes

You can make a bubble wand out of almost anything—you just need a frame to hold a film (very thin layer) of bubble before you blow air into it. Here are a few ideas, but you can come up with plenty more of your own. You need wide, shallow bowls for the bubble mix; wide enough to dip your wand into.

Chenille stems (pipe cleaners)

To get different shapes, bend the stem a little in the middle and, starting from the middle, wrap it around a cookie cutter or a small box or pot. When the two ends meet, wrap one around the other so you have a handle.

To make them even prettier and stronger, twist two different colored stems together before you start, or you could thread pony beads onto the handles.

Drinking straw

Take a drinking straw and a sharp, pointy pair of scissors. At one end, cut four slits at 90 degrees to each other (at 12, 3, 6, and 9 o'clock on a clock face), each about ¾ in. (2 cm) long. Splay out the ends into a propeller shape.

Plastic bulb pipettes

These bubble wands are used in some of the projects. You can buy the pipettes inexpensively from drug stores (pharmacies), hobby stores, or online—they have lots of different uses. For a bubble wand, simply snip off the bulb (wide part), dip that end in your bubble mix, and blow through the narrow end.

Paper

Take two sheets of printer paper, roll them into a cone, and secure with sticky tape. Cut a little off the sharp end to blow through. Trim the wide end so that the cone is about 3–4 in. (8–10 cm) long. To cut it, flatten the end a little, but don't crease it. Cut it smoothly so there are no raggedy bits and the end is a perfect circle.

Plastic bottle

Use a sharp pair of scissors to cut the base off a plastic bottle. Ask an adult to help you cut it completely smooth. Put the wide end into the bubble mix and blow through the neck.

Wire coat hanger or garden wire

For a big wand, pull a coat hanger into the shape you want. Ask an adult to help you straighten the hook with pliers and wrap it round a stick handle. Bind it on with ribbon or twine. Use garden wire for a smaller wand.

LET'S INVESTIGATE

Some people say you need a material to wick (suck up) bubble mix to make bigger and better bubbles, so bubble wands made out of string, paper, or chenille stems (pipe cleaners) work better than plastic or wire ones. Is this true? Does wrapping your wire bubble wand in cotton string make it work better?

Bubble Mixes

What you need

- About ½ cup (250 ml) warm water
- 1 tablespoon glycerin or granulated sugar
- 2 tablespoons dish soap (washing-up liquid)
- Plastic wrap (clingfilm)

It is easy to make bubbles. You do it every time you wash the dishes or have a shower and wash your hair, but in this chapter we are aiming to make BIG bubbles and strong, long-lasting bubbles, and for that you will need to start mixing and investigating, using one of these recipes, until you get the mix that works best for you. There are thousands of recipes on the internet if you want to keep experimenting.

A simple bubble mix for smaller bubbles

1 Pour the water into a bowl. Add the glycerin or sugar and the dish soap. Stir slowly and smoothly until all the sugar has dissolved. Try not to make any foam on top.

2 Cover the bowl tightly with some plastic wrap and let it rest for several hours. (The longer you leave it, the better the bubbles—24 hours is good if you can wait that long.)

What you need

- ½ cup (65 g) corn starch (cornflour)

- 6 cups (1.5 liters) water

- ½ cup (250 ml) dish soap (washing-up liquid)

- 1 tablespoon glycerin

- 1 tablespoon baking powder

- Plastic wrap (clingfilm)

A bubble mix for really big bubbles

Put the corn starch into a large bowl or pitcher (jug) and gradually add water, stirring it into a paste and then into a runny liquid. (Corn starch slime is a strange material which is worth investigating another time.) Now add all the other ingredients and stir slowly and gently to avoid making any froth. Cover with some plastic wrap and leave for 24 hours. (It will work before that, but leaving it for longer makes for better bubbles.)

Top Tips for Perfect Bubbles

- Stir your ingredients together slowly and smoothly to stop foam forming on the top.

- Water from the faucet (tap) is usually fine for bubbles, but if you live in an area with very hard water (where you get lots of limescale in your kettle and shampoo doesn't lather well), distilled water will be better.

- Some dish-washing detergents are better than others (see page 7). Use the basic liquid—not special bio, perfumed, or moisturizing ones.

- Be patient and wait—if possible, make your bubble mix 24 hours before you need to use it.

- Have all your containers and spoons clean and grease-free—bubbles hate grease.

- Cloudy, humid days are better for bubbles than dry, sunny ones.

The Science of Bubbles

Before we start experimenting with bubbles—blowing them, changing their shape, making them float, and more—it will help if you understand how bubbles work. In order to do this, try this experiment where there are no bubbles at all!

What you need

- Glass of water
- Scrap of toilet tissue one layer thick
- Thin needle
- Dropper or pipette

1

Fill the glass with water and float the scrap of tissue on the surface.

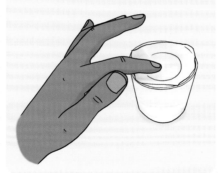

2

Gently place the needle on the tissue.

LET'S INVESTIGATE

To look for surface tension, try using a dropper to drop water on different surfaces. On some surfaces the drop spreads out or soaks in. On others it bunches up into a tight round dome. Which surface works best for holding water drops?

3

Watch as the tissue sinks and the needle is left floating on the surface.

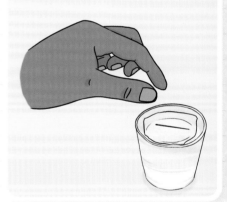

Inside the science

It seems impossible that a metal needle can float, but it does because of surface tension. You can see surface tension on a pond where little bugs, called pond skaters, run over the water without sinking. Look closely at their feet and you will see six little dips, as if they are standing on a skin on the water. You can also see the effect of surface tension in drops of water, especially on leaves after rain.

How a water drop forms

We can understand surface tension by looking at how water molecules behave. Each molecule holds on tightly to the molecules around it with an attraction that is a bit like a magnetic force. In the middle of the water drop, each molecule is pulled in all directions equally but in the top layer, next to the air, they are only pulled from underneath and to the sides.

So the top molecules are pulled inward and become like a tight skin, which the needle will float on, and pond skaters can walk on, and which pulls a drop into a dome. (If a water drop spreads out, the water is attracted to the surface it is put on and this attraction is stronger than the pulling-in force of surface tension.)

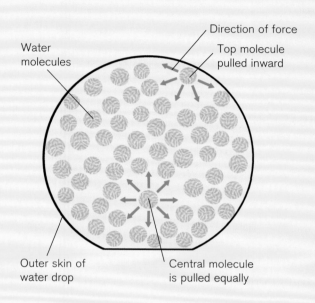

Water molecules

Direction of force

Top molecule pulled inward

Outer skin of water drop

Central molecule is pulled equally

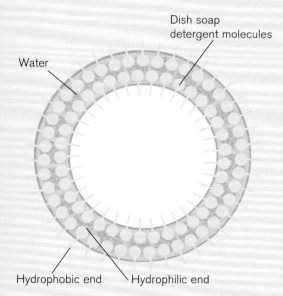

Dish soap detergent molecules

Water

Hydrophobic end   Hydrophilic end

How a bubble forms

So what is this to do with bubbles? A bubble blown in plain water instantly pops because the water molecules pull back together into a drop, away from the air. You need to add dish soap (detergent), as its molecules have special properties. One end is attracted to water (they are hydrophilic, which in Greek means water lover) and one end wants to get away from water (they are hydrophobic, meaning water hater). When you add detergent, the molecules mix with the water molecules, but the water-hating ends try to get away into the air at the surface. They get between water molecules so they can't hang onto each other—the surface tension is broken. However, in a water drop there is not enough space for them all to touch air.

In a bubble, a very thin layer of water is sandwiched between two layers of detergent molecules. All the molecules pull together into a sphere and many more can touch air, either inside or outside the bubble. The bubble will pop when the water evaporates. Adding glycerin (or corn/golden syrup or sugar) slows down this evaporation and makes the bubble last longer.

Big Wands for Big Bubbles

What you need

Simple version

• Yarn (about 6 times the length of one straw)

• Wooden skewer (which will fit through the straw)

• Sticky tape

• 2 drinking straws

• Bubble mix (see page 19)

• Wide, shallow container

Have you ever seen a street performer creating giant bubbles? They look really tricky, but we've given you some easy instructions on how to make big wands to blow big bubbles, just like the professionals!

How to make a simple big bubble wand

1

Overlap the end of the piece of yarn over the end of the skewer by about 1 in. (2.5 cm). Wrap it with sticky tape to hold it in place.

2

Push the skewer through each straw in turn to thread them onto the yarn. Unstick the yarn from the skewer, remove the skewer, and knot the yarn ends together to make a loop.

3

Slide the straws along the yarn so you can pull them apart to make a rectangle, with the straws at the sides and yarn between them.

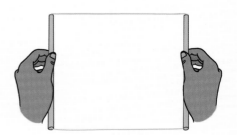

4

Hold the straws together and dip them in the bubble mix. As you raise your arms and walk backward, slowly pull the straws apart and the bubble film will fill with air.

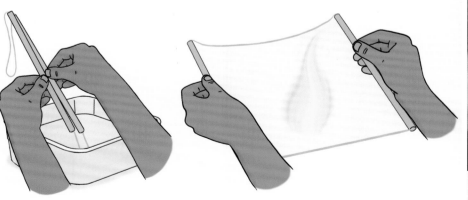

What you need

Tri-string version

• 2 screw eyes (a closed loop with a screw threaded base)

• 2 dowel rods as handles, about 12–16 in. (30–40 cm) long

• Baker's twine (cotton string), about 4 ft (1.2 m) long

• 2 metal washers or a hex nut as a weight

• Bubble mix (see page 19)

• Wide, shallow container

How to make a tri-string wand

1

Ask an adult to help you screw a screw eye into one end of each of the dowel handles. Cut a 16-in. (40-cm) length of twine or string and tie it to the screw eyes between the dowel rods.

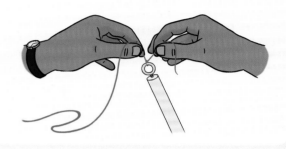

2

Cut a 32-in. (80-cm) length of twine or string and thread the washers or nut onto it. Tie the ends of the twine to the screw eyes. When you hold the handles up and pull them apart, you will have a triangle-shaped loop of string.

3

With the handles held together, dip the twine into your container of bubble mix and lift the wand up high. Spread the handles apart to let the bubble start forming (you may have to walk forward or backward if there is no breeze).

4

To close and free the bubble, bring the handles in together again.

TOP TIP

Remember, it doesn't matter how long your string is, so long as the bottom string is twice as long as the top one This tri-string wand is a small one for beginners. You can work up to a bigger one—like the professionals use—as you get more experienced.

Inside the science

To make really big bubbles, you need a lot of bubble mix. You must start with a wand that has a big hole in it or something like twine or string to soak up more bubble mix, so the bubble can keep growing.

Even with the simple, rectangular bubble wand, or the triangular tri-string wand, you probably didn't blow a cube- or triangle-shaped bubble. Small, free-flying bubbles are always spheres. This is because the water and detergent molecules which make up the soap film (see page 21) are all pulling together and each one of them has an equal amount of pulling power. They pull into the most symmetrical shape you can get—a sphere. The molecules would go on pulling together until they were just a drop of bubble mix, but the air inside stops them.

Bubble Colors

What you need

- Bubble mix (see page 18)
- Simple round bubble wand (see page 16)
- Transparent plastic lid (from a yogurt pot or potato chip tube)
- Sticky tape
- Flashlight (torch)
- Spoon
- Drinking straw or pipette bubble wand (see page 16)

Now let's think about the color of bubbles. One reason everyone loves bubbles is because they are so delicate, shimmery, and beautiful, but have you looked at a bubble really closely to see what makes it so special?

1

Start outside in the daylight. Blow some bubbles using a simple round bubble wand and catch one back onto your wand. Look for two reflections—one the right way up and the other upside down. Watch closely for swirling colors, too.

2

Now go into a dark room (with the light on at first). Tape the plastic lid onto the front of the flashlight, with the rim up, like a shallow bowl. Hold the flashlight upright with the lid on top.

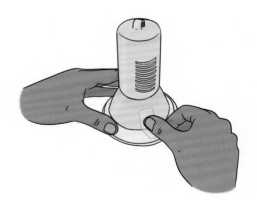

3

Use your finger to wet the plastic lid with bubble mix, including around the rim, and then put a spoonful of mix into the lid. Use the straw or pipette bubble wand to blow one big bubble dome to cover the lid.

4

Turn the lights off and the flashlight on. Hold the flashlight with the bubble in front of your face and look up into the bubble. Can you see all the colors of the rainbow? Perhaps not all of them and, if you watch very closely, the colors you see may change before the bubble pops. What patterns of color do you see?

LET'S INVESTIGATE

Try to record which colors you can see and how they change—using a voice recorder might be the easiest way. Experiment with different-colored cellophane under the transparent lid. What does this do to the colors? Also try different light sources. Do LED torches give you different colors than old-fashioned filament torches?

5

Now dip the straw or pipette wand in bubble mix, push it inside the bubble, and blow gently —watch as the colors change and swirl around.

Inside the science

Find a shiny spoon and look into it; your reflection is upside down. Turn it over and look at the back; your reflection is the right way up. A mirror that curves in (concave) gives an upside-down reflection. The inside of the bubble is curved in like this. Light passes through the transparent (see-through) outside of the bubble and reflects off the inside surface on the opposite side—this makes an upside-down reflection. But some light also reflects off the bubble's outside surface, which curves out (convex), and this gives a reflection that is the right way up, like the one on the back of your spoon.

All the different colors you see in the bubble are because light is made up of all the colors of the rainbow. Each color has a different wavelength. Remember that the

bubble film is a sandwich of water molecules between dish soap molecules (see page 21). When white light hits the soap film, some reflects off the outer layer of soap molecules and some off the inner layer a tiny distance away. This means that the wavelengths of the different colors in the two reflections are slightly out of step, as one had further to travel, and so they "interfere." Some waves cancel each other out; some get together and are stronger—these are the colors you can see.

As water evaporates from the bubble, the space between the two layers gets thinner so that some wavelengths interfere and you see different colors. When they are about to pop, they look black. Moving air also changes the thickness.

Floating Bubbles

Bubbles will fly away in the wind, but in the end they will either pop or fall back to earth, where they will burst when they touch the ground. Well, not always. Look what happens to the bubbles in this project.

What you need

• 2-quart (2-liter) clear soda bottle

• Scissors

• Tablespoon

• Vinegar

• Baking soda (bicarbonate of soda)

• Bubble mix (see page 18)

• Bubble wand (see page 16)

1

Take any labels off the bottle and then cut off the top so that you have a clear, straight-sided container.

2

Pour 2 tablespoons (30 ml) of vinegar into the bottle and add 1 tablespoon of baking soda (bicarbonate of soda).

Inside the science

When you mix vinegar and baking soda (bicarbonate of soda) together there is a chemical reaction that produces the gas, carbon dioxide.

Carbon dioxide is heavier than air so it stays at the bottom of the bottle. When you blow bubbles into the bottle, they start to drop down—this is because of gravity. However, the air inside the bubbles is lighter than the carbon dioxide, so the bubbles float on it and appear to hover.

LET'S INVESTIGATE

Do large bubbles hover better than small ones? How long do they hover before they drop into the bowl?

3

Stand the bottle upright on a flat surface and watch as the two ingredients react together and foam up in the bottle.

4

When the reaction has died down, blow some bubbles into the bottle using a simple bubble wand and some bubble mix. Watch the bubbles hover in the air— why aren't they dropping down?

Square Bubbles

Bubbles are always spheres, we proved that on page 21, except now we're going to show you how to make a square-shaped, or rather a cube-shaped, bubble!

What you need

- 6 drinking straws
- 6–9 chenille stems (pipe cleaners)
- Scissors
- Lots of bubble mix (see page 18)
- Large, deep container for the bubble mix—at least 3 in. (7 cm) across and 3 in. (7 cm) deep
- Pipette bubble wand (see page 16)

1

First, make a cube with the straws and chenille stems. Cut the straight parts of the straws into 3-in. (7-cm) lengths (throw any bendy parts away); you need 12 pieces. Cut the chenille stems into 4-in. (10-cm) lengths; you also need 12 of these.

2

Push a chenille stem piece into each straw. Slide the straw to the center and bend up the ends of the chenille stem so the straw stays in place.

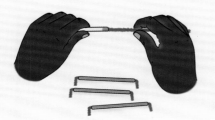

3

Hold two straws side by side and twist the chenille stems together. Pull the straws to make a right-angle corner. Stand a third straw upright at the corner and twist the protruding stem from this around the join. Put this to one side and take three more straws and do the same again. Do it twice more so you have four pieces each with three arms—the corners of your cube.

4

Now twist two ends of two 3D corners together, and add the remaining 3D corners to connect the sides of your cube.

5

Fill your container with bubble mix and dip the cube into it so that it goes right under. Pull it out by one corner. As you pull it out you will see bubble films stretched between the edges of the cube. Give it a little shake and you will see them link together. A square window of bubble film will appear in the center. Shake it around a little and it will change from vertical to horizontal or horizontal to vertical.

LET'S INVESTIGATE

Make some different 3D shapes with straws and chenille stems to blow different-shaped bubbles—for example, you could try a triangular pyramid.

6

Put the cube on a flat surface with the square window horizontal. Take the bubble wand and blow a bubble. Shake it so the bubble falls onto the square window. Shake the cube gently and your round bubble will join with the square window to make a cube-shaped bubble (with slightly curved faces). This may take a bit of practice!

7

Try making the bubble bigger. Take the bubble wand and dip it into the bubble mix so it is wet all over the bulb. Slowly push it into the cube-shaped bubble and blow.

Inside the science

We found out on page 21 why bubbles are spherical. What happens in this experiment is that the soap film clings to the sides of the cube, pulling at the bubble. These soap films use the shortest possible distance while still connecting all the sides, which pulls the sphere into a cube. But the bubble is still trying to be a sphere so the sides are bulging.

Bubbles Inside Bubbles

· ·

If you touch a bubble, it will pop—true? False! You can push things right inside bubbles and they won't burst. This is what you're going to do in this activity: It takes a bit of skill and patience but has amazing results.

What you need

• Smooth surface, such as a kitchen counter top or a plastic tray

• Bubble mix (see page 18)

• Pipette bubble wand (see page 16)

• Drinking straw

1

Clean your smooth surface with some of your bubble mix; make sure there are no dips, bumps, grease spots, or crumbs. Now spread a circle of bubble mix on the surface with your fingers.

Inside the science

2

Use the pipette bubble wand to blow a large half bubble (hemisphere) onto the wet circle.

Anything dry is a bubble's arch enemy! Imagine two friends holding your hands and pulling you in opposite directions. You will stay still. If one lets go, you'll be pulled straight into the other friend. Water molecules in bubbles are being pulled from both sides. When the bubble lands on a dry surface, there are no water molecules pulling from the dry side so the edge of the bubble is pulled away from the surface toward the center and it bursts. The bubble doesn't pop on the wet counter top or with the wet pipette because the molecules still have "friends" on both sides!

3

Dip the straw into the bubble mix—you could use the pipette again but the straw may work better. Carefully push the straw through the first bubble (if the straw is wet with bubble mix, the first bubble shouldn't burst), and slowly blow another bubble. Watch what happens to the first bubble as you blow.

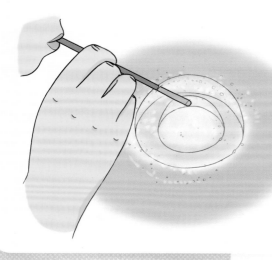

4

Repeat the process, pushing your straw through the two bubbles before you blow the next. Keep going!

LET'S INVESTIGATE

How many bubbles within bubbles can you make? What happens to the outside bubble each time you add another bubble? Try wetting a long nail or needle with bubble mix and pushing it right through the bubble. Can you do the same with your finger?

Bubble Tennis

Have you ever tried to catch a bubble? The chances are that as soon as you touched one it popped. Here is a clever way of catching a bubble and seeing it bounce. Why not play bubble tennis, bouncing it to a friend? You could add multiple players and make up your own bubble game.

What you need

• Pair of clean knitted gloves (one glove for each player)

• Bubble mix with glycerin (see page 18)

• Bubble wand (see page 16)

1

Each player puts a knitted glove on one hand. Blow a few bubbles and hold out your gloved hand to catch one. It won't pop, it will bounce.

LET'S INVESTIGATE

Experiment with different types of gloves—try latex, cotton, wool, or leather—then try different bubble mixes: remember the bubble only lasts until the water in it evaporates, so mixes that slow down evaporation will work best (see page 37).

2

Bounce it on to a friend to play bubble tennis, or simply bounce it from hand to hand. How many pats can you give it before it bursts?

Inside the science

Grease, oil, and dirt are all bubble busters!
The water molecules in a bubble hate grease and pull away from it, bursting the bubble Our hands are naturally slightly oily, so if a bubble touches your skin it bursts. Gloves provide a barrier between the bubble and your skin. Bubbles also pop when water evaporates from them. The glycerin in the bubble mix slows down evaporation so the bubbles last longer for your game.

Bubble Prints

This is a very simple activity that combines art, science, and math. The delicate bubble prints are a beautiful way of decorating card or paper for greeting cards or thank-you notes, and while you are about it do a little investigating. There are two different techniques to try here. Which one gives you the best results?

What you need

- Food coloring or acrylic (poster) paint
- A few shallow bowls
- Dish soap (washing-up liquid)
- Tablespoon
- Drinking straw
- Paper—strong absorbent paper or card works best
- Pipette (optional)

For the investigation:

- Transparent plastic document wallet
- Scissors

1

Place a squirt of food coloring or paint into a bowl. Add a tablespoon of dish soap and a little water. Mix together well.

LET'S INVESTIGATE

Cut the top off the document wallet about halfway down, so that the pocket you have left is a bit shorter than a straw. Pour a little bubble mix into the wallet and use a straw to blow bubbles until they rise up into the wallet. Now examine the different shapes you can see.

2

Use the straw to blow into the paint mix until you have a good mound of colored bubbles in lots of sizes.

Hold the paper flat over the bubbles, gently touch the paper on the bubbles, and lift it straight off again. Examine your print. Keep experimenting with the amount of paint, water, and bubble mix to get the clearest prints. You can build up layers of different colors using different bowls for each color. Look carefully at the shapes of the bubble prints you have captured. Are they round?

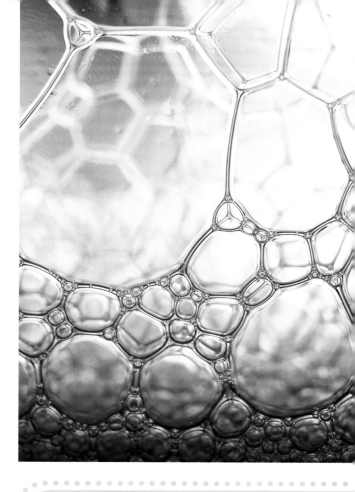

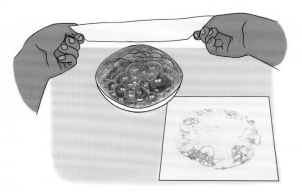

Variation

Another technique is to start with just bubble mix in a clean bowl. Blow a good mound of bubbles and use the pipette to drop a little food coloring or paint on top. Use different colors in different places. The color will collect around the edges of the bubbles. Lay a sheet of paper on top and lift it up to reveal your multicolored print. Keep experimenting to get the best prints.

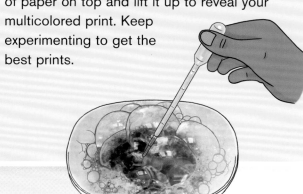

Inside the science

When two bubbles meet, they join so that they share the wall between them. If the bubbles are the same size, the wall will be flat. Smaller bubbles are at higher pressure than larger ones, so a small bubble will bulge into a bigger one. Where three bubbles join, the angle between the walls will always be 120 degrees. This is the angle inside a regular hexagon. Look at the bubble prints or the bubbles sandwiched in the plastic wallet, and you will see that some of the bubbles form a pattern a bit like a beehive, with hexagon-shaped faces. It is a very efficient shape.

Chapter 2

Bubbling Brews and Fizzing Foams

In this chapter, you will be investigating different types of bubbles and how they appear as gases or are mixed inside different liquids to make foam. Bubbles are cool in chemistry: whenever you mix two or more different ingredients and you see bubbles, you know a reaction is happening and new materials are appearing. Foams are fascinating, too. They are bubbles of gas trapped in a liquid, which behave a bit like a solid. Try these experiments to find out more!

Glowing Lava Lamp 42

Pop-up Glove 46

Rainbow Snake 49

Elephant's Toothpaste 52

Shaving Foam Marbling 55

Bobbing Raisins 58

Soda Geyser 60

Fizzing Rocks 62

Bubbling Pondweed 64

Amazing Bubble Wrap 67

Glowing Lava Lamp

What you need

- Drinking glass
- Bottle of vegetable oil
- Teaspoon
- Funnel
- Water
- Clear plastic bottle
- Food coloring
- Alka-Seltzer tablets (or fizzing Vitamin C tablets)
- Glow stick (optional)

You'll soon be hypnotized watching the bubbles rise through the oil in this beautiful lava lamp. If you make your lamp after dark, drop in a glow stick, switch off the lights, and you will have an even more magical experience.

1

Before you start making your lava lamp, have a bit of fun investigating oil and water. Fill a glass with water and then drop in a teaspoon of oil. Watch what happens to the oil. Stir it hard to mix it into the water and then wait and watch! You should see all the oil coming together and making circles, which are like two-dimensional bubbles on the water. When they meet, they join together.

TOP TIP

If you don't have a glow stick, use a flashlight (torch) and either (very carefully!) rest the bottle on the flashlight, or tape the flashlight behind the bottle.

2

Now make your lamp. Using the funnel, pour water into the bottle until it is about a quarter full.

3

Using the funnel again, pour in the vegetable oil until the bottle is a bit more than three-quarters full. You need to leave room for your glow stick.

LET'S INVESTIGATE

Does the lamp work better with bigger pieces of tablet? Try adding a little of another type of vegetable oil or baby oil. Does it make another layer in the bottle?

Inside the science

Oil and water don't mix and oil floats on top of water because oil is less dense than water. (If you have the same volume of oil and water, the oil will weigh less than the water.) Oil forms circles on top of water because of surface tension (see page 21).

Oil molecules are hydrophobic (they hate water). The oil molecules pull together so that there are as few as possible in contact with the water molecules. This makes a circle. Different circles of oil are attracted to each other and join into a bigger circle.

When you drop the piece of Alka-Seltzer into the lava lamp bottle, it drops through the oil and into the water. It doesn't react with the oil, but it does with the water. It begins to fizz, releasing small bubbles of carbon dioxide gas. These bubbles get attached to blobs of water and act like floats (like in the bobbing raisin experiment on page 58). The blobs rise up to the surface through the oil. When they reach the surface, the gas escapes and without its float to hold it up, the denser water sinks back down.

4

Watch as the oil and water separate into two layers, with the heavier water sitting at the bottom. Wait until the oil and water have settled.

5

Add about 12 drops of food coloring. Watch as it falls through the oil—the coloring will not mix with the oil. It will fall until it meets the water and will then sit on top of the water for a few seconds before bursting and spreading out. Gently twist the bottle a few times to help the color mix with the water, but don't stir or shake it.

6

Now, break an Alka-Seltzer (or fizzing Vitamin C) tablet into about 4 smaller pieces. Drop one piece of the tablet into the bottle. It will drop through the oil into the water and begin to fizz. Watch as bubbles begin to erupt through the oil. When the bubbling starts to slow down, add another piece of Alka-Seltzer and it will start all over again.

7

For the full glow show, bend your glow stick to activate it, drop it into the bottle, and switch off the lights.

What you need

- 3 sticky labels
- 3 small transparent plastic cups (the gloves should fit tightly over the top of the cups)
- Active dried yeast (for baking)
- Teaspoon
- Sugar
- Water
- Measuring pitcher (jug)
- Spoon for stirring
- Waterproof tray
- 3 latex gloves (the type doctors use)

Pop-up Glove

Yeast is used to make bubbles in bread dough (see page 80), but it is a bit like Goldilocks in the story of the Three Bears. It doesn't like things too hot or too cold; they need to be just right! You can see this by watching the gloves in this experiment. In the right conditions, the yeast produces carbon dioxide gas that will inflate the glove to make a pop-up hand on top of the cup!

1
Use the sticky labels to label the cups 1, 2, and 3.

2
Put one teaspoon of dried yeast into each cup. Each teaspoon of dried yeast contains millions of microscopic yeast cells!

3
Add two teaspoons of sugar to each cup.

4

Ask an adult to boil some water in a kettle and then let it cool for about 5 minutes so that it is still quite hot, but not boiling.

5

Measure ½ cup (100 ml) of cold water into the measuring pitcher (jug), pour it into cup 1, and stir it well.

6

Now measure about ⅓ cup (70 ml) of cold water into the pitcher (jug) and then very carefully add hot water until you have ½ cup (100 ml). The water should be cool enough to put your finger into comfortably. Pour this into cup 2 and then stir well.

7

Lastly, very carefully measure ½ cup (100 ml) of hot water and pour it into cup 3. Stir it well.

8

Making sure that you don't spill the mixture, carefully put a glove over the top of each cup. Stand the cups together on a tray.

Inside the science

The water activates the dried yeast, bringing it back to life (because all living things need water).
The yeast then feeds on the sugar and, as a waste product, produces carbon dioxide, which inflates the glove. Yeast needs to be at a certain temperature to be properly alive and active—the best temperature is 105–115°F (41–46°C). Very hot water will kill the yeast. In cold water it activates very slowly.

9

Now you need to wait. Watch carefully to see if you can spot any bubbles forming in the mixtures or any froth on the top. Froth will show that the yeast is feeding on the sugar and making bubbles of carbon dioxide. Keep checking every 10 minutes to see what is happening. You could leave the experiment for several hours or even overnight. Which of the gloves do you think will pop up? How long does it take? What do you think might happen to the yeast in cup 3 with the very hot water? What do you think will happen with the cold water?

LET'S INVESTIGATE

Using warm water in all three cups and the same amount of yeast in each, try the experiment again with different amounts of sugar in each cup. Add another cup with no sugar to see if the yeast really needs the sugar. Or, use warm water in all three cups and the same amount of sugar in each, but put different amounts of yeast in each cup.

Rainbow Snake

Bubbles can be huge and pop very easily, or they can be tiny and all joined together, and so strong you can make different shapes with them; that's what foam is. There's lots of fun to be had making this foam snake—how long can you keep blowing?

What you need

- Sharp scissors
- Plastic bottle
- Wash cloth or a square of old towel
- Large elastic band
- Food coloring in assorted colors
- Wide bowl
- Dish soap (washing-up liquid)
- Water

1 Use the scissors to cut the bottom off the plastic bottle.

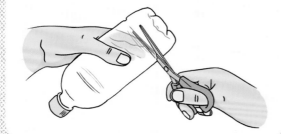

2 Cover the open end of the bottle with the wash cloth and hold it in place with the elastic band.

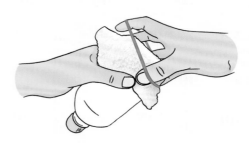

3 Dot food coloring in a circle around the tight edge of the wash cloth (we've used lots of colors here, but using just two or three colors is fine). Squirty bottles are easiest for this or use a clean teaspoon for each color.

4

In the bowl, mix up two or three tablespoons of dish soap with a little water. Dip the wash cloth end of the bottle into the soap mix—it needs to be wet but don't leave it there too long or you'll wash the colors out.

5

Hold the top of the bottle to your lips and blow. Keep blowing—you will blow a long snake of tinted rainbow foam out of your bottle.

Inside the science

Foam is still a bit of a mystery to scientists. Foam is mostly gas (95%) inside a small amount of liquid (5%) and yet it keeps its shape like a solid. How the foam behaves depends on the way the bubbles stick together or slip past each other. Look carefully at your foam—the bubbles aren't spheres but flat-sided 3D shapes with faces, with shapes like hexagons and pentagons.

LET'S INVESTIGATE

Does a stronger solution of dish soap with less water make better foam? What happens if you use different fabrics instead of the wash cloth? How long does your snake last?

TRY THIS!

This experiment is just as impressive without the rainbow effect. Simply dip the cloth-covered end in bubble mix and blow until you have a long snake of foam, or something that resembles and elephant's trunk! Try bottles in different sizes for thicker or thinner snakes, too.

What you need

- Safety goggles and latex gloves
- Clean, empty 16 fl oz. (500 ml) plastic bottle
- ½ cup (250 ml) 6% hydrogen peroxide liquid (from drug stores/pharmacies)
- Large waterproof tray to catch the overflowing foam
- Dish soap (washing-up liquid)
- Food coloring (optional)
- Tablespoon
- Warm water
- Small cup
- 1 package of active dried yeast
- Funnel

Elephant's Toothpaste

This well-known experiment definitely has the wow factor, but you will need an adult to help you with it as it uses a chemical (hydrogen peroxide), which can irritate the hands and eyes. Put on protective goggles before you start, then stand back and be amazed as foam pours out of the bottle, a bit like toothpaste fit for an elephant.

1 Put on the goggles and gloves. Ask an adult to pour the hydrogen peroxide into the bottle. Protect your surface with a tray.

2 Add about 1 tablespoon of dish soap into the bottle and swish the bottle around a bit to mix it. If you want colored toothpaste, add a few drops of food coloring.

3 Put about 3 tablespoons of warm water into a cup and sprinkle on the yeast. Stir it together for about 30 seconds until the yeast has dissolved.

4 To save mess, go outside or keep the bottle on the tray. Put the funnel in the top of the bottle and pour in the yeast mixture. Quickly take out the funnel, stand back, and watch as foam pours out.

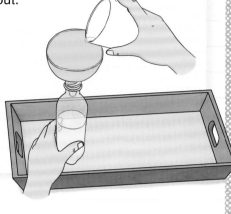

Inside the science

The bubbles in this foam are different from any other bubbles we have looked at so far, because they are full of oxygen, not air or carbon dioxide. Everyone knows that the chemical formula for water is H_2O. That means each molecule of water has two hydrogen atoms and one oxygen atom. The formula for hydrogen peroxide is H_2O_2, which means it has an extra oxygen atom, which can quite easily be pulled off as oxygen gas, leaving water (H_2O) behind. The yeast in the elephant's toothpaste acts a catalyst (a chemical that helps a chemical reaction happen, though it doesn't change itself), removing the oxygen very fast so it creates lots of bubbles very quickly and produces heat at the same time, so the bottle should feel hot when you touch it. At the end, all that is left in the bottle and on the tray is a mixture of water, soap, oxygen, and yeast, so you can safely pour it down the drain.

5 After watching for a while, feel the bottle—is it warm or cool?

LET'S INVESTIGATE

Does the experiment work as well with cold water? Does more yeast produce more foam? How could you measure if more foam is produced?

Shaving Foam Marbling

Like the bubble prints on page 38, this is another great way to combine art and science. The colored prints produced in this way are much stronger than for bubble prints. Don't use your dad's best shaving foam for this—buy bargain foam with no added moisturizers or gels.

Like the bubble prints on page 38

What you need

- Piece of vinyl tablecloth (oilcloth) or sheet of thick plastic
- Shaving foam
- Baking pan
- Acrylic paint and/or food coloring
- Toothpick or wooden skewer
- Thick paper or cardstock
- Timer or clock
- Squeegee

1

Spread out the piece of vinyl tablecloth on your work surface. Squirt a thick layer of foam into the pan.

2

Dot drops of paint or food coloring onto the foam. Use two or three different colors.

3

Swirl the dots into patterns using the toothpick or skewer. Don't mix them too much—you want the colors to stay separate.

4

Place a sheet of paper over the foam and press down lightly. Peel off the paper and lay it flat on the vinyl tablecloth. Let it rest for about 3 minutes (use a timer) for the color to soak into the paper.

5

Use the squeegee to scrape off all the foam onto the vinyl mat. Place the marbled paper somewhere flat while it dries.

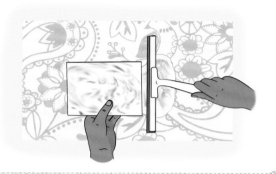

Inside the science

The two ends of soap molecules are very different (take a look at the Science of Bubbles, on page 20). One end is hydrophilic, and likes to attach to water molecules, and the other end is hydrophobic, and moves away from water molecules. Food coloring and acrylic paints are both colored dyes mixed with water. The hydrophobic ends of the soap molecules in the shaving foam do not want to attach themselves to the watery paints. On the other hand, the molecules in paper are hydrophilic—that's why paper absorbs water. So when you put the paper on the foam, the paint transfers easily to the paper, and spreads across it, creating patterns you didn't see in the foam.

6

Lift the vinyl tablecloth to the sink and wipe off the foam before starting again. Swirl your foam to make another pattern or add more color.

LET'S INVESTIGATE

Try these artistic investigations: Do you get different effects from food coloring and acrylic paint? Is it best to flatten your foam or leave it in mounds and troughs?

What you need

- Bottle or can of soda (fizzy drink)—it is easier to see with a clear drink, such as lemonade
- Tall, clear glass
- Raisins

Bobbing Raisins

This is a really simple, quick experiment, but you will be transfixed by the bubbles for a long time. See if you can work out what is happening before you read about the science behind it, and you can do the experiment and still drink the soda afterward!

Open the bottle or can of soda. Watch (and listen) as bubbles begin to rise to the surface. Pour some soda into a tall glass. Drop a handful of raisins into the glass. Watch them carefully. After a few seconds they begin to dance—rising to the surface and then dropping back again.

Inside the science

The bubbles in soda are carbon dioxide. Carbon dioxide is forced into the bottle or can in the factory at a high pressure and this pressure makes it dissolve in the water so that it is invisible. When you take the top off the bottle, or open the can, the pressure drops and the carbon dioxide comes out of the water in bubbles. Bubbles form more easily on the bumpy surface of the raisins where there are tiny air pockets. As more and more bubbles attach themselves to the raisins, they begin to act like floats, carrying the raisins up to the surface. There the bubbles burst and, without their floats, the raisins drop back down to the bottom and the whole process starts again.

LET'S INVESTIGATE

Does the size of the raisins matter? Use jumbo raisins, ordinary raisins, and currants so that you have three different sizes to try. Drop in other things, such as rice or dried pasta. What happens? Is there a difference with cold and room-temperature sodas? Try the experiment using a screw-top jar instead of a glass. What happens if you put the lid on the jar?

Soda Geyser

There are some places in the world, such as Iceland, New Zealand, or Yellowstone Park in the USA, where, every few hours, or in some cases minutes, huge geysers of hot water and steam shoot into the air. Making your own geyser with candy and soda is not quite so dramatic, but it comes close (and has some interesting science behind it). This is an experiment that is much easier to do with a friend.

What you need

- Empty 2-quart (2-liter) soda bottle

- Tube of Mentos

- Some paper or Steve Spangler's Geyser Tube Kit (available online)

- Sticky tape

- 2-quart (2-liter) bottle of diet soda (use diet not regular soda so it doesn't leave a sticky mess)

1

The hardest part of this is to drop at least six Mentos into the soda all at the same time! You can practice your technique with an empty soda bottle before you begin. Cut some paper to the length of the Mentos tube then roll it around the tube and secure it with some sticky tape.

TOP TIP

Don't attempt this experiment inside! Find a big outdoor space, like a lawn or field away from other people and animals.

2

Open the Mentos, put your finger over the bottom of the tube, and drop six Mentos into the tube so that they are piled on top of one another. Hold the tube over the empty soda bottle, remove your finger, and watch the Mentos drop into the bottle. Practice until it is easy!

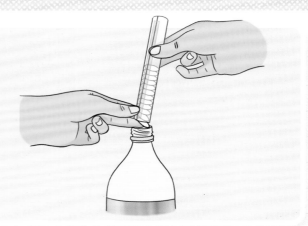

3

Take the full soda bottle and six Mentos in the paper tube to the middle of a large open space. Stand the bottle on the ground. If it is wobbly make a small mound of soft dirt or sand to stand it in. One person takes the top off the bottle, and the other person immediately drops in the Mentos from the paper tube. Then both of you run backward quickly, watching the bottle all the time for the whoosh!

LET'S INVESTIGATE

To do investigations on your geyser you will need lots of bottles of soda and lots of Mentos, and you will need to find a way of measuring how high it spurts, which can be tricky. Try setting up a tripod and taking a video with the camera in an identical position and pointed at an identical angle each time. Or, put the geyser against a tall wall and see how high the wall gets wet.

Try using different numbers of Mentos, different types of (diet) soda, or different temperatures of soda. To make a fair test in science remember to only change one thing at a time (see page 9). So, you could get three bottles of the same soda, keep it at the same temperature, and do the experiment with 3, then 6, then 9 Mentos and see if there is any difference in the results.

Inside the science

This is a bit like the bobbing raisins experiment on page 58, except that everything happens much more quickly and dramatically. Just like raisins, on Mentos there are thousands of microscopic pits all over the surface and bubbles can form very quickly on these. As soon as the heavy Mentos drop into the soda, they sink to the bottom and bubbles form all over them. These rise quickly to the surface. The great rush of bubbles from the bottom pushes all the soda out of the bottle in one enormous geyser.

Fizzing Rocks

Have you ever wondered why there are so many different-colored pebbles, or been amazed by the layers of rock you can see in a dramatic canyon? If so, perhaps you are a budding geologist—someone who studies rocks. This next activity uses bubbles to help you identify rocks, just like a geologist.

What you need

- Lots of different rock samples
- Tray
- Vinegar
- Pipette or teaspoon
- Magnifying glass
- Piece of eggshell

1

When you are out and about, look for rocks or pebbles with different colors and textures. Collect small samples—you don't want to be hauling around a heavy backpack.

2

Start with a hardness test. Some rocks are much harder than others, with diamond being the hardest! Try scratching one piece of rock with another. The harder one will always make a scratch on the softer one. Start with two and test them. Then take another rock and test it with the one that came out hardest. Is this new one harder or softer? Gradually sort out your rocks from hardest to softest, lining them up along a tray.

3

Now for the bubble test. Drop a little vinegar (a weak acid) on the rock with a pipette or teaspoon and watch for fizzy bubbles using the magnifying glass. Bubbles are a sign that a chemical reaction is taking place. If you see bubbles you can identify your rock as one that contains carbonates, like chalk, limestone, and marble. (If you have lots of vinegar and small pieces of rock you could put the rock in a bowl and cover it with vinegar instead.)

LET'S INVESTIGATE

Acid, such as vinegar, reacts with some rocks and gradually dissolves it. When rain falls through air polluted by car exhausts, smoke from fires, and gases from factories, it becomes acidic and it wears away (erodes) marble and limestone on buildings. So when you are out and about, look at old buildings, statues, or gravestones to see if they have been damaged by acid rain. The statues often lose their faces first.

4

Now put a few pieces of eggshell in a cup with a little vinegar and watch for bubbles.

Inside the science

Some rocks contain the mineral calcium carbonate. When this is mixed with acid there is a chemical reaction and carbon dioxide gas is released, making bubbles. Chalk and limestone are both sedimentary rocks, which means they were formed from everything that fell to the ocean floor millions of years ago (called sediment), including the shells and bones of ocean creatures. Over time the sediment was pushed together to form rock. Chalk is a special type of limestone formed from the shells of microscopic creatures called coccoliths, which lived in the age of the dinosaurs. These prehistoric shells contain calcium carbonate just like the eggshell. Marble is a metamorphic rock (which means "changed structure"). It is formed when limestone is compressed (squashed) and heated to high temperatures by movements of the earth's crust. It is much harder than chalk and limestone which are quite soft and crumbly, but still contains calcium carbonate.

Bubbling Pondweed

What you need

• Oxygenating pondweed, such as elodea

• Clean, clear glass jar— a tall narrow one is best

• Pitcher (jug) of water

• Flat-bottomed bowl

• Timer

Scientists are always interested when bubbles appear from nowhere because it means something is going on! In the 1770s, a Dutch scientist called Jan Ingenhousz noticed that when plants were underwater and in sunlight, they produced bubbles. If they were in shade there were no bubbles. What was going on? Try this experiment on a sunny day to find out!

1

Do this first part in the sink. Take a piece of the pondweed and put it upside down in the jar. Fill the jar to the very top with water from the pitcher, so the water is bulging over the glass.

STAY SAFE

Take care when collecting pondweed. Kneel at the pond edge and do not stretch out too far. Always have an adult with you when near water.

2

Put the bowl upside down on top of the jar. Press the bowl down firmly so it is sealed against the jar and turn the two over together. The bowl will now be the right way up and the jar upside down in the bowl. If you do this carefully, no water will spill out of the jar and there should be no air in the jar.

3

Add water to the bowl until it comes about halfway up the side of the jar.

Inside the science

All living things need food but plants don't eat or get food through their roots—they make their own food by photosynthesis (which means "making with light"). Inside every green leaf there is a chemical factory that uses water sucked up from the plant's roots and carbon dioxide from the air to make glucose (sugar). Chlorophyll (the chemical that make leaves green) lets plants absorb the energy from the sun to make this possible. Oxygen is a waste product of photosynthesis. You can see the oxygen being produced by water plants because it makes bubbles, but all plants are producing oxygen whenever there is enough light. This is lucky for us because we need oxygen to stay alive. Most of the oxygen in the air is produced by plants; about half by land plants and half by microscopic plants called phytoplankton in the oceans.

4

Carefully carry your bowl and jar to a really sunny place, either outside or inside by a sunny window. Now start to watch for bubbles. Use your timer and try and count how many rise to the top in 1 minute. The bubbles will be very small. Do this several times.

5

Leave the bowl in the sun for a few hours and then look at the jar. Has the water level dropped a little? What has replaced the water?

LET'S INVESTIGATE

After the jar has been in the sun for a while, move it into the shade. Leave it there for about 5 minutes and then try counting bubbles again. Do the bubbles stop? Move it back into the sun. How quickly do they start again?

Amazing Bubble Wrap

The bubbles in bubble wrap are made in a factory, so why include them in this chapter? Well, we can use bubble wrap to understand how bubbles act as a thermal insulator to keeps things warm (or cold), in the same way that foam is used to insulate a building. We can also find out how well bubble wrap protects an egg from breaking!

1

First measure a piece of bubble wrap to cover one of your eggs so that it looks like a wrapped hard candy. Being very careful not to break the egg, wrap it around the egg once with a small overlap, and make sure it is long enough to gather up the ends and seal them with an elastic band.

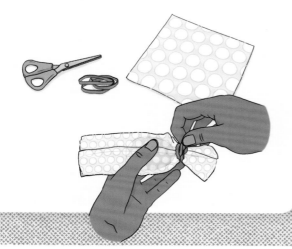

2

Unwrap the egg. Now ask an adult to help you boil five eggs in a pan until hard cooked—boil them for about 12 minutes (use a timer).

Inside the science

Heat is a form of energy that travels through materials at different speeds.
For instance, heat travels through metal quickly, so you would soon burn your hand if you stirred a pan with a metal spoon. How quickly heat travels depends on the way the molecules are arranged. The energy of heat makes molecules move. In solids they vibrate and bump into the molecules next to them, making these vibrate, so heat travels quickly. In liquids, molecules are spread further apart so it takes a little more time. In gases, the molecules are even further apart, so gases make good thermal insulators. Bubble wrap traps air (a gas) in pockets and foam traps it in bubbles, so heat energy takes longer to travel through, which means they are both good thermal insulators. This works for cold objects, too—an ice cube wrapped in a thermal insulator will stay cold longer as the outside warmth doesn't travel easily through to the ice.

Air is also a good packing material because it squashes. The molecules are a long way apart so they can be pushed closer together. When you drop the egg, the energy from the ground hitting the bubble wrap squashes the air rather than breaking the egg.

3

While the eggs are boiling, use the measured piece of bubble wrap as a template to cut out pieces of bubble wrap from the remaining two sheets, so you have three pieces with different-sized bubbles. Cut two pieces of plastic wrap that are the same size as the bubble wrap pieces.

4

When the eggs are cooked, cool them in a pan of cold water for a couple of minutes until they are cool enough to handle.

5

Wrap up three of the eggs in different types of bubble wrap and one in two layers of plastic wrap—this makes it a fairer test because the bubble wrap has two layers. Leave one egg without any wrapping: this is called a control and is there to see if eggs stay hot without any wrapping.

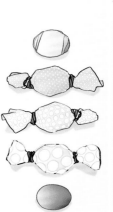

6

Leave all the eggs together in one place, but not touching each other so they can't keep each other warm.

7

After about half an hour, open the wrapping a little and stab each egg in turn with the meat thermometer to find the temperature of the egg right in the middle. Which one has stayed warmest? Did the plastic wrap without bubbles keep the egg any warmer than no wrapping at all?

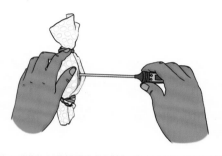

8

Now for the part that could get messy! Use all the rest of your bubble wrap to wrap up the last uncooked egg. Secure it with elastic bands and sticky tape so you have a fat package. Now stand on a chair and drop it—did the egg break? Unwrap it and see. If it is still whole, wrap it up again and drop if from somewhere higher. Did it survive?

LET'S INVESTIGATE

Will shaving foam insulate an egg in the same way as bubble wrap does? Try it. Support the egg on a couple of pieces of modeling clay so that you can put foam underneath it as well as all around it. Remember to compare it with a control egg with no foam and with your best bubble wrap. Look for solid foams around your house. You'll find foam insulation around water pipes and tanks. Polystyrene is a type of foam that is used for packaging and to insulate floors, roofs, and walls, and takeout cups (styrofoam). Some houses have liquid foam pumped into their walls which expands and sets hard, creating insulation.

Chapter 3

Cooking with Bubbles

Perhaps you are thinking, "What is a cookery chapter doing in a science book?" The answer is, cooking IS science! Every time you cook you are causing a chemical reaction and changing an ingredient into something different. The chemical reactions that make bubbles and foams are used in some of our favorite foods, including bread, cake, meringue, pancakes, and whipped cream. So, enjoy making, eating, and finding out about the science through tasty bubbles and foams.

Remember to put on an apron and wash your hands well with soap and warm water before you cook, and ask an adult to help before you use the stove or any electrical equipment.

Whip that Cream 72

Honeycomb Toffee 74

Animal Bread Rolls 78

Bubbling Breakfast Pancakes 82

Erupting Pans 85

Light-as-air Meringues 88

Baked Alaska 92

Whip that Cream

Have you ever wondered how runny cream turns into a soft light foam of delicious whipped cream that can be enjoyed on desserts? Well, it's all about the bubbles!

What you need

- Carton of whipping cream
- Mixing bowl
- Rotary hand whisk (or an electric beater)

1 Pour the cream into the bowl and start whisking. Ask an adult to help if you are going to use an electric beater. A rotary hand whisk is more fun and you can feel how much energy is needed to whip the cream.

2 Stop whisking every 10 seconds and see what is happening to the cream. At first you will just see some bubbles which rise to the surface and pop. Next, you will see streaks in the cream, then soft little mounds sitting on the surface. At some point you will see more cream in the bowl and it formed into peaks that hold their shape. The cream feels solid. It's ready to blob on your strawberries or spread on your pie!

LET'S INVESTIGATE

What happens if you keep beating the cream after it has thickened? Try it and see. Keep on beating and you will find that the foam begins to deflate and lumps appear which stick to your whisk. That's butter! The watery liquid is buttermilk, which you can use in cooking. Place a strainer over a bowl and strain off the buttermilk. Press all the butter lumps together with the back of a spoon, squeezing out the buttermilk, and use it on your bread.

Inside the science

Cream is the fatty part of milk together with water (and some sugar and protein). Fat is hydrophobic—it hates water and won't mix with it—but there's another chemical in cream which, a bit like detergent (see page 21),  has one end attracted to water (hydrophilic) and the other end which hates water (hydrophobic). The fat is held in drops surrounded by this chemical with the hydrophobic ends facing in toward the fat and the hydrophilic ends toward the water.

When you beat the cream this protective layer gets broken and also air gets pushed into the cream. The fats try to clump together away from water, but when they can't find another fat molecule they grab onto air molecules instead (anything rather than water), creating air bubbles in the cream. Lots of air bubbles make foam and that's what whipped cream is.

TOP TIP

Watch carefully as you whip the cream and stop when you have a soft foam that holds together. Don't overwhisk (see above)!

What you need

- Butter, for greasing
- 1 ½ teaspoons baking soda (bicarbonate of soda)
- ½ cup (100g) superfine (caster) sugar
- 4 tablespoons corn (golden) syrup

- Baking sheet
- Kitchen foil
- Paper towel
- Small bowl
- Large, heavy-based pan
- Candy thermometer
- Wooden spoon
- Glass of cold water
- Rolling pin

Honeycomb Toffee

Honeycomb, or sponge toffee, is sweet, sticky, and delicious! It's great fun to make your own—the mixture explodes into a bubbling foam when you add the baking soda. This recipe looks a bit like a mad science experiment—you will be using chemical reactions to produce gas, to make candy!

STAY SAFE

It is most important that you ask an adult to help you with this recipe, as hot sugar can cause very bad burns. Put on an apron and wear a top with long sleeves in case the toffee splashes your skin. Your adult helper should do the same.

1

Cover the inside of the baking sheet (bottom and sides) with foil and then use a piece of paper towel to rub butter all over it to stop the honeycomb sticking.

TOP TIP

Always remember to clean your teeth thoroughly after eating delicious, sticky honeycomb!

2

Measure the baking soda into a small bowl and put it to one side for later. Put the sugar and corn syrup in the pan and ask an adult to help you place it on the hob over a low heat. Stir occasionally with a wooden spoon until all the sugar has melted and you can no longer feel any grittiness at the bottom or side of the pan. Put the candy thermometer into the pan.

3

Now the adult must take over. Stand back and watch as she turns the heat up. The mixture will begin to bubble and boil and turn a light amber color. The adult should not stir it again, but she should check the temperature on the thermometer. It needs to reach 300°F (150°C), which will take less than 3 minutes.

4

When the temperature is getting close to 300°F (150°C), the adult should take the pan off the heat and use a wooden spoon to drop a little of the mixture into a glass of cold water. If the toffee is ready, it will harden into brittle threads, which break when you take them out of the water. This is called the hard crack stage. If the threads are soft and bendy, the toffee isn't ready and needs to be boiled for a little longer before being tested again. Be careful at this stage, as it is very easy to burn the mixture.

5

As soon as the toffee is ready, take it off the heat and let the bubbles die down a little. The adult should tip in the baking soda and stir it into the bubbling sugar, making sure it is well mixed. The toffee will rise up in the pan making a dramatic, golden foam.

6

Straightaway, the adult should pour the honeycomb onto the baking sheet before it begins to harden in the pan. Let it cool completely.

7

Turn the honeycomb out onto a clean surface and peel off the foil. Hit it gently with a rolling pin to break it up into little pieces.

8

To clean up, put the pan, the spoon, and thermometer into a large sink full of water and leave it until the hard toffee dissolves, which doesn't take long.

Inside the science

When you heat the sugar and syrup (which is another type of sugar), the sugar melts and the water in the syrup evaporates changing how it behaves. You need to heat it to 300°F (150°C) because sugar that has reached this temperature and is then cooled quickly becomes a brittle solid (hard toffee). This is why you drop it into water to test it. (At lower temperatures it will make soft toffee when it cools.) Usually you add acid to baking soda to make it release carbon dioxide gas but in this recipe it is the heat that makes it happen.

When you stir in the baking soda, the carbon dioxide immediately bubbles through the liquid sugar making it look like lava from a volcano. When you pour the mixture into the tray, the sugar quickly hardens and traps the bubbles in a solid foam.

LET'S INVESTIGATE

The bubbles in the honeycomb came from carbon dioxide gas, produced in a reaction triggered by heat. Combining baking soda (bicarbonate of soda) with acid is another way to make carbon dioxide bubbles (see page 30). What liquids found in your kitchen will cause a reaction? Put a teaspoon of baking soda into each of few plastic beakers and add a little liquid to each. Try different fruit juices, milk, runny yogurt, soda, wine (ask an adult first), or ketchup. Any liquid that produces bubbles is a weak acid.

Animal Bread Rolls

What you need

- 1⅔ cups (250 g) unbleached all-purpose (plain) flour
- 1 level teaspoon salt
- 1 level teaspoon sugar
- 1 level tablespoon soft butter
- 1 package active dry yeast
- ⅝ cup (150 ml) warm water (hot water will kill yeast. If the water is too hot for your little finger, it is too hot for the yeast)
- Butter, for greasing the baking sheets
- A few raisins for eyes
- Baking sheet
- Mixing bowl

Good bread is all about the bubbles. It is exciting to make bread because it is made with yeast and yeast is alive. As yeast grows, it makes bubbles of carbon dioxide gas in the dough and that's why bread has holes in it. Watch your dough rise and double in size before your eyes as the yeast works its magic. Then make cute animal-shaped rolls—a delicious treat eaten warm with a filling of your choice.

1

Put on an apron and wash your hands well with soap and warm water.

2

Prepare the baking sheet by putting some butter on a paper towel and rubbing it lightly over the sheet. This is called "greasing." It will stop the rolls from sticking to the sheet.

3

Put the flour into the mixing bowl. Add the salt and sugar and mix everything together with your hand.

4

Add a tablespoon of butter and rub it into the flour between your fingers and thumb until it is all mixed in and the mixture is crumbly, like breadcrumbs. Pour in the yeast and mix it in well.

5

Make a hollow in the middle of the flour mixture. Pour the warm water slowly into the hollow so that it makes a pool within the flour.

Inside the science

Water activates the yeast, bringing it back to life.

The yeast uses the sugar and flour as food and releases carbon dioxide as a waste product (see page 48). When you knead the dough, you fold it to trap air and squeeze it to help form long strings of protein from the flour, called gluten. Gluten is elastic. When you stretch it, it pulls back toward its original shape. Fill it with air or carbon dioxide and it makes bubbles. The carbon dioxide, produced by the yeast, joins into any bubbles it finds in the dough—making them bigger—and the dough grows and grows. When you put the bread in a hot oven, the gas in the bubbles expands so the bubbles get even bigger and the bread rises some more. The dough cooks and hardens in the oven with the bubbles trapped inside.

6

Using your hand, gradually stir the flour into the water—the mixture will turn from a runny mixture to a soft dough as more flour is mixed in. Work the dough with your hand until all the flour has been mixed in. (If there are dry crumbs in the bowl and the dough feels very dry and hard to mix, add a little more water to the bowl, one tablespoon at a time. If the dough is very sticky and sticks to your fingers or the sides of the bowl, add more flour, one tablespoon at a time.)

7

Sprinkle a little flour over the work surface and tip the dough out of the bowl onto the surface. Using both hands, knead the dough. To do this, push the ball of dough down and away from you with the heel of your hands, stretching and flattening it as you push. Fold the far edge toward you. Turn the ball around half a turn and stretch the dough out again. Fold and turn again. Keep doing this for about 10 minutes— you'll soon get into a rhythm. It's hard work, but you can take a short rest every now and then. You'll know when the dough is ready because it will begin to feel soft and springy in your hands. Feel how it stretches and then pulls back like elastic.

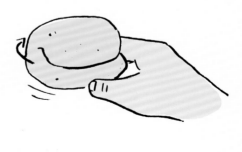

8

Divide the dough into even pieces. Make each piece into an animal shape, using raisins for the eyes. You could make crocodiles, mice, cats, pigs, snakes, or hedgehogs (make the spikes by cutting snips into the dough with kitchen scissors). Place the animal rolls on the baking sheet, spaced well apart.

9

Cut a piece of plastic wrap (clingfilm) more than big enough to cover the baking sheet. Spread the plastic wrap out on the work surface. Put a few drops of oil onto some paper towel and wipe this all over the plastic wrap. Cover your rolls with the plastic wrap, oily side down. Tuck it around the sides (this will prevent the rolls from drying out).

10

Leave the tray in a warm place (near a warm stove or above a radiator) for the dough to rise. After about half an hour, your rolls will have doubled in size.

11

While the dough is rising, ask an adult to help you turn on the oven to 425°F (220°C/Gas 7).

LET'S INVESTIGATE

What happens if you don't place the rolls in a warm place? Make another batch of dough and divide it into equal balls. Place each one on a small plate and cover with oiled plastic wrap. Put them in different places, some warm, some cold, including one in the fridge! After half an hour compare how big they have grown. Before you bake them, let them rest for at least another half hour in a warm place so the yeast in the cold ones has time to work.

12

When your animals look nice and plump and the oven is hot, ask an adult to help you place the baking sheet into the oven. Bake until the rolls are golden brown—about 15–20 minutes, depending on the thickness of the rolls. Again with adult help, carefully remove the sheet from the oven and tip the rolls onto a wire rack to cool.

What you need

- Scant 1 cup (135 g) all-purpose (plain) flour
- 1 teaspoon baking powder
- ½ teaspoon salt
- 2 tablespoons superfine (caster) sugar
- ½ cup (130 ml) milk
- 1 US extra large (UK large) egg, lightly beaten
- 2 tablespoons butter, plus extra for frying
- Maple syrup

- Sifter (sieve)
- Large mixing bowl
- Lidded microwave-safe bowl
- Skillet (frying pan)
- Spatula

Bubbling Breakfast Pancakes

Weekends should begin with a special breakfast and pancakes make the best start to the day. But what good are breakfast pancakes without bubbles? Make this delicious recipe for light, fluffy pancakes and watch for the bubbles as you cook.

1

Set a sifter (sieve) over a large mixing bowl and sift the flour, baking powder, salt, and sugar into the bowl. Break the egg into another bowl or pitcher (jug) and add the milk. Whisk them together.

2

Put 2 tablespoons of butter into a small microwave safe bowl with a lid and microwave it on full power for about 30 seconds. Carefully check to see if the butter has melted or nearly all melted. Stirring should finish off the melting but you can microwave for another 20 seconds if you need to. Whisk the melted butter into the egg and milk.

3

Pour the egg mixture into the flour and use a fork to beat it until you have a smooth batter. There will be lumps at first but they will disappear if you keep beating. Let the batter stand for a few minutes before you begin cooking the pancakes. The mixture is quite thick.

4

Put a knob of butter in a skillet or frying pan and ask an adult to help you heat it over a medium heat. When the butter has melted, tip the pan in each direction to make sure the butter has covered the bottom and then use a ladle to pour some mix into the pan. If your pan is big enough you could cook two or more pancakes at the same time.

5

Now watch for bubbles! When you see bubbles at the top of the pancake use a spatula to flip it over. The bottom should be a golden brown. Cook until the other side is the same color and the pancake (which is now full of bubbles) is about ½ in. (1 cm) thick.

Inside the science

This recipe uses baking powder not baking soda (bicarbonate of soda). Baking soda is made only of sodium bicarbonate, which immediately releases bubbles of carbon dioxide when an acid such as vinegar is added to it (see page 30). Baking powder contains not only sodium bicarbonate but also two acids in powder form. It only begins to bubble when it gets wet and one of the acids dissolves. This was happening when you let your batter rest. The second acid needs the heat of cooking to make it react, so more bubbling takes place in the pan. Gradually the liquid foam becomes a solid foam as the batter mix cooks, trapping all the bubbles.

6

Keep making pancakes until all the batter is used up. Keep them warm in the oven (set to low) or make them to order for your family, with the last ones kept for you. Serve them with more butter and lots of maple syrup.

LET'S INVESTIGATE

One way to investigate the power of bubbles in breakfast pancakes is to make pancakes without adding baking powder. Made with flour, milk, and eggs, these will turn out as "flat as a pancake!" These are the kind of pancake you make on Shrove Tuesday (Pancake Day)—try flipping them in the pan to turn them over. You can easily find a recipe on a cooking website.

Erupting Pans

Your family probably boils a kettle or pan of water many times every day, but have you ever thought about why bubbles appear when you boil water? What happens with other liquids, such as pans of thick soup?

What you need

- Kettle
- Non-stick pan
- Can/carton of your favorite thick soup
- Wooden spoon
- Safety goggles
- Oven mitts

1

Ask an adult's permission and then fill a kettle with water and set it to boil. Close your eyes and listen very carefully. Note how the sounds change as it heats up. Can you hear when it is about to boil?

2

Ask an adult to help you, then put some water in the pan and set it on the stove to heat up. Keep away from the steam, but carefully watch the bubbles in the water and how they change. Keep listening, too. Can you match what is happening in the pan to the changes in the sounds you hear as the water comes to the boil?

3

Now ask an adult to empty the water out of the pan (they could use it for tea of coffee) and pour in the soup instead. Make sure you are wearing an old top with long sleeves and put on an apron, safety goggles, and oven mitts.

4

Heat the pan over a low heat, stirring it once every now and then to stop the soup sticking to the pan and burning. Watch carefully but keep back. As the soup gets hotter, bubbles erupt on the surface and splash soup everywhere. It looks like the boiling mud you get in volcanic places, like New Zealand or Yellowstone Park in the USA. Watch this happen for a few seconds and then stir to stop you and your kitchen getting into a soupy mess. When the soup is steaming, pour it into a bowl or mug and drink it.

LET'S INVESTIGATE

Try boiling milk (this is messy and you will need to clean your stove top afterward!). What do you notice that is different to boiling water? As you heat the milk, water evaporates from the top, leaving a creamy lid of fat on the surface. Underneath this, bubbles of water vapor collect in a thick layer of foam. Eventually this foam lifts the top, creamy layer up the pan and breaks through—and all the foamy milk spills over the edge. Keep well back and ask an adult to take the pan off the heat as soon as the milk has boiled over. Could you predict when the milk was going to erupt?

Inside the science

Water has lots of air dissolved in it, which is why fish can breathe in water. Cold water can dissolve more air than hot water, so when the water temperature rises, the air comes out in bubbles. These are the bubbles you see around the sides of the pan when you first start heating the water. Then, as the temperature reaches boiling point at 212°F (100°C), the water turns into a different type of bubble—water vapor—which rises rapidly in the boiling water and escapes as steam.

Bubbles in water escape very quickly because water molecules move around easily. Soup is much more viscous (thicker). This means the molecules hold together more tightly. Bubbles of water vapor in the soup need much more pressure inside them before they burst, so you get a violent explosion—which can splatter soup everywhere. It's a bit like the difference between blowing a bubble until it pops and blowing up a balloon until it pops. If you stir soup as you heat it, it all warms up evenly, spreading the heat so it doesn't boil and splutter.

What you need

- 4 US extra-large (UK large) eggs

- 1 cup plus 2 tablespoons (225 g) superfine (caster) sugar

- A little lemon juice

- 2 baking sheets

- Baking parchment

- Paper towel

- China, glass, or stainless steel mixing bowl (not plastic)

- Small china plate

- Egg cup

- Rotary hand whisk (or an electric beater)

Light-as-air Meringues

Here's a recipe that uses air bubbles beaten into egg whites to make crunchy meringues. You can then sandwich the meringues together with more air bubbles trapped inside the soft, whipped cream from page 72. You can also use this recipe to make the meringue for the Baked Alaska on page 92.

1

Ask an adult to help you turn on the oven to 275°F (140°C/Gas 1). Cut two pieces of baking parchment to fit the baking sheets.

2

Wipe the inside of the mixing bowl and the plate with a squeeze of lemon juice on some paper towel to make sure that they are completely grease-free. Wash your beaters in hot soapy water and then rinse and dry them well.

3

Separate the egg whites from the yolks. To do this, carefully break one egg at a time onto the plate, place an egg cup over the yolk, and let the white slide off into your grease-free mixing bowl. If you do break the yolk of an egg do not use that egg white—it may spoil your meringue! (You do not need the yolks for this recipe, so put them into another bowl to use for something else.)

4

Stand the bowl on a damp cloth to keep it from wobbling as you whisk the eggs. If you have a rotary hand whisk it is fun to use this, otherwise ask an adult to help you use an electric beater. Watch as the slimy whites begin to break up and go a bit bubbly and then turn to a white foam. Keep whisking until they turn stiff. You'll know if you have whisked enough when you lift out the whisk and there are sharp little peaks of white standing up in the bowl.

TOP TIP

Eggs from the fridge are easier to separate, but let the whites reach room temperature before you beat them.

5

Now add 1 heaped tablespoon of the superfine (caster) sugar and whisk it into the egg white, then add another one and whisk again. Keep going until you have whisked in all the sugar and have made a stiff, glossy meringue.

6

Stick the baking parchment to the sheets with a tiny blob of meringue in each corner. Now use a metal spoon to make 16 rough blobs of meringue, eight on each tray, spaced well apart.

7

Ask an adult to help you put the sheets in the oven and bake for 1½ hours until the meringues are a light brown and sound crisp when you tap them. Then turn off the oven but leave the meringues inside for 4 more hours to cool slowly—this will make them really crisp and crunchy.

8

Sandwich two meringues together with whipped cream (see page 72), so that you have 8 meringue treats in total.

LET'S INVESTIGATE

When you are beating the egg whites, as it begins to fluff up, take out half a teaspoon every 10 seconds or so (including after you have added each tablespoon of sugar), and drop it onto a plate to see how long the egg white keeps its shape. This shows you why beating long enough is so important. Does the sugar make a difference to how strong the foam is? See what happens if you keep beating the egg whites after they have reached the sharp peak stage (without adding sugar). Can you beat an egg too much?

Inside the science

Egg white is almost all water (90 percent) and the rest is mostly different types of protein. Some of these protein molecules are hydrophilic (they love water) and some are hydrophobic (they hate water). Normally in egg white the hydrophilic proteins surround the hydrophobic ones and protect them from the water.

When you beat the egg white you push air into it and you also break apart some of the proteins. The hydrophobic ones move toward the air bubbles to get away from the water. The more you beat the egg, the more protein-surrounded bubbles are made so the whole thing fluffs up. Adding sugar helps to keep the foam strong while you cook it—and it tastes nice! Any fat, including any trace of egg yolk, will stop the proteins lining up around the air bubbles so your meringue will be flat.

Baked Alaska

What you need

For the sponge cake

• ¾ cup plus 2 tablespoons (115 g) all-purpose (plain) flour

• 1 teaspoon baking powder

• ½ cup plus 1 tablespoon (115 g) superfine (caster) sugar

• 1 stick (125 g) unsalted butter, very soft

• ½ teaspoon vanilla extract

• 2 US extra-large (UK large) eggs

• 1 tablespoon milk

• Round cake pan, 8 in. (20 cm) diameter

• Baking parchment

• Baking sheet

• Mixing bowl

• Sieve

For the filling

• 1 pint (500 ml) strawberry ice cream (or your favorite flavor)

• 1½ cups (150 g) raspberries

For the meringue

• 4 US extra-large (UK large) eggs

• 1 cup plus 2 tablespoons (225 g) superfine (caster) sugar

A hot, meringue-topped cake with a freezing ice cream surprise inside—that's what a Baked Alaska is and bubbles make it possible! The meringue here is cooked very quickly, so it is soft and light.

1

Ask an adult to help you turn the oven on to 350°F (180°C/Gas 4). Put the pan on the baking parchment and draw around it. Cut just inside the line to make a disk of paper. Put a little soft butter on a piece of paper towel and rub it around the inside of the cake pan. Fit the parchment disk into the base of the pan and put it to one side.

2

Put a sifter (sieve) over a mixing bowl and sift the flour and baking powder into the bowl. Stir in the sugar, then add the very soft butter and vanilla extract.

3

Break the eggs into a small bowl. Pick out any pieces of shell, then add the milk and lightly beat them with a fork to break them up. Pour the eggs into the mixing bowl. Beat all the ingredients together with a wooden spoon (or ask an adult to help you use an electric beater), until the mixture is very smooth and light. Spoon the mixture into the prepared cake pan and spread it evenly around the pan.

4

Ask an adult to help you put the sponge cake in the preheated oven to bake for about 25 minutes, until it is a light golden brown. To test if the cake is baked, ask an adult to help you remove it from the oven and gently press it in the middle. If it springs back it is baked; if there is a dimple, then bake for 5 minutes more. Let it cool for a couple minutes, then run a round-bladed knife around the inside of the pan to loosen it and carefully turn out the cake onto a wire rack. Leave it to cool completely.

Inside the science

Making a Baked Alaska uses lots of science ideas we have already met in other projects (see the pancakes on page 82 and meringue on page 88). What happens in a Baked Alaska is the same as what happened with the bubble wrap on page 67. Air is trapped in the foam of the meringue and the bubbly sponge of the cake. Remember, air is a good thermal insulator. The heat from the oven takes a long time to travel through the cake and the meringue, giving the meringue a chance to cook a little before the ice cream melts.

5

When the cake is cold, remove the ice cream from the freezer and leave it until it is soft enough to scoop out easily. Put the sponge cake onto a baking sheet, then scoop or spoon the ice cream on top and spread it out to make an even layer using a palette knife. Work quickly so it doesn't melt. Put the whole thing back into the freezer and leave it until the ice cream is very firm— at least 1 hour, but you can leave it in the freezer for up to 3 days.

6

When you are ready to finish the Alaska, ask an adult to help you turn the oven on to 425°F (220°C/Gas 7), which is very hot.

7

Now follow the recipe for meringue on page 89, starting at step 3 and ending at step 6, when you have a bowl full of meringue.

8

For the next stage, you need to work really quickly so that the ice cream stays frozen hard. First, check that the oven is very hot then remove the sponge and ice cream from the freezer. Quickly spoon the raspberries all over the top of the ice cream.

9

Still working very fast, cover the whole cake with the meringue, spreading it all over the top and sides of the cake, right down to the baking sheet. Make a few peaks in the topping. The meringue stops the ice cream from melting, so there must be no holes or gaps!

10

Ask an adult to help you put the Alaska in the oven to bake for just 4–5 minutes, until it is lightly browned. Any longer and the ice cream will melt. Serve immediately!

LET'S INVESTIGATE

What other materials keep things cold? Wrap some ice cubes in different materials—bubble wrap, plastic wrap, foil, fleece fabric. Leave one ice cube without any wrapping. Which ones will stay frozen longest? When the unwrapped one has nearly melted, check the wrapped ones—which ones have melted least?

Chapter 4

Balloon Magic

~~~~~~~~~~~~~~~~~~~~~~~~~~~~

Balloons make people smile and seem to say, "Come and celebrate!" but there is also a lot of science you can find out from balloons. Most balloons are made from latex, which comes from the sap of rubber trees. Latex is elastic—when stretched, it tries to pull back. You can use the stretchy nature of a balloon to weigh air, demonstrate how your lungs work, investigate different gases, and observe how heat is absorbed by color. Pretty cool stuff for a party decoration!

What's that Wailing? 98

How NOT to Pop a Balloon! 100

Skewer a Balloon 102

Balloon Rocket 104

Electric Balloon 107

Black and White Balloons 110

Balloon Fire Extinguisher 112

Hovering Helium 116

How Your Lungs Work 118

Weighing Air 122

What's that Wailing?

It's fun to do this experiment with friends. Find out who can get their coin spinning the fastest and loudest!

What you need

- Large balloons—light colored, almost transparent ones are best
- Small coin
- Balloon pump
- Small metal hex (hexagonal) nut

1

First, put the coin inside a deflated balloon.

2

Now inflate the balloon, as big as it can safely go, and tie it off with a knot.

3

Hold the balloon upside down, with the knot under your palm. If the balloon slips, lick your fingers—they will stick. Now move the balloon around in a circle as if you were stirring a cake mix but much faster. You want to get the coin spinning around the edge of the balloon in a big circle. It takes a bit of practice.

4

Once the coin is spinning, hold the balloon still and watch the coin keeping spinning… and spinning… and spinning… How long does it keep going? What can you hear?

LET'S INVESTIGATE

Do small coins or large ones spin for longer?

What happens with bigger or smaller hex nuts or balloons—do you hear different notes?

What happens if you put in more than one coin or hex nut?

Inside the science

The coin or nut keeps spinning in a circle because of centripetal force, which means center-seeking force. The famous scientist, Sir Isaac Newton, explained it in his "first law of motion:" That a moving object keeps going in a straight line at the same speed unless another force acts on it. Our coin or hex nut is not going in a straight line, it's going in a circle. Something must be making that happen and we call it centripetal force.

The coin looks like a planet orbiting the sun and that's because planets are held in position by centripetal force, otherwise they would fly off into space—the coin would do the same if the balloon popped. Gravity holds planets in place; for the coin it is to do with the way it bounces on the sides of the balloon. The coin or nut slows down and falls eventually because of gravity, but it keeps going for a long time because the inside of the balloon is so smooth there isn't much friction to slow it down. The hex nut makes the weird sound because it vibrates against the balloon and vibrations cause sound waves.

TRY THIS!

Take another balloon and put the hex nut inside this one. Again, blow it up, nice and big, and tie it off. Spin this one in the same way—listen and feel the vibrations.

How NOT to Pop a Balloon!

What you need

- Safety goggles
- Balloons
- Balloon pump
- Thumb tacks (drawing pins)

Popping a balloon is easy—just push a pin into it. But what happens if you push it down onto lots of pins? If you don't like popping balloons, get some help while you cover your ears!

1

Inflate two balloons. Put on your safety goggles. Put one thumb tack point up on a hard surface. Push balloon number 1 down onto the thumb tack. Get ready for the pop!

2

Now take a handful of thumb tacks—they must all be identical. Turn them all point up on the surface and gather them together into a small group.

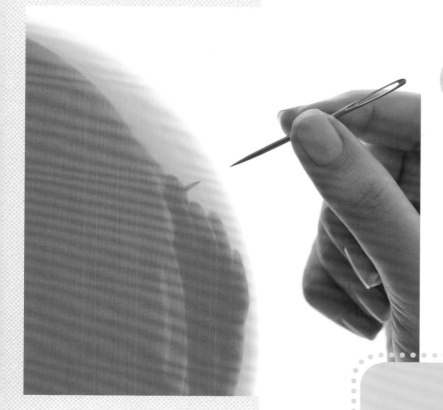

The balloon pops with one thumb tack but doesn't pop with lots. How many thumb tacks do you need to have before it doesn't pop? To make it a fair test you need the same push on the balloon each time. Try putting the same heavy book on the balloon to push it onto the thumb tacks.

3

Take balloon number 2 and push it down onto the thumb tacks. Push harder. How hard do you need to push before the balloon pops?

Inside the science

If you push a balloon down onto one thumb tack, all the force is on one tiny point, which easily makes a hole in the stretched rubber. Push the balloon onto lots of thumb tacks and the force is shared between lots of points, so the force with which each one pushes into the balloon is much less and is spread over a wider area: There isn't enough force to pop the balloon. Think about if you wanted to hammer a post into the ground. A flat wide end would be very difficult to hammer in, but a pointed end would go in easily because all the force is on a tiny spot.

Skewer a Balloon

Prick a balloon with a pin and it pops, so how is it possible that can you push a skewer right through a balloon without it bursting? Find out here, but take care with the sharp skewer.

What you need

• Small balloons—the skewer should be longer than the balloons

• Balloon pump

• Long bamboo skewer

• Sandpaper

• Dish soap (washing-up liquid) or cooking oil

• Safety goggles

1

Inflate a balloon until it is quite big and then let about a third of the air out before you tie it off.

2

Use the sandpaper to smooth off and sharpen the point of the skewer. Rub a little dish soap or cooking oil over the tip of the skewer to lubricate it (make it slippery).

3

Put on your safety goggles. Slowly push the skewer into the side of the balloon—does it pop?

4

Inflate another balloon. Still wearing your safety goggles, slowly but firmly push the skewer into the balloon just beside the tied-off neck, twisting it a little from side to side as you push. It should push through. Keep pushing the skewer right through the balloon to the very bottom and push it out of the other side. The balloon will stay inflated. You can even pull the skewer out and the balloon will only deflate slowly.

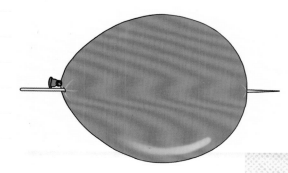

LET'S INVESTIGATE

Use a marker pen to draw dots about ½ in. (1 cm) diameter all over an uninflated balloon. Make sure you make some around the neck and one at the very bottom. Inflate the balloon and look at what happens to the dots. Now can you see why you can skewer a balloon?

Inside the science

Balloons are made of latex and the molecules in latex are in long strands that stretch when you inflate the balloon. Look at the pattern of dots you made in "Let's Investigate" and you can see they have stretched a lot at the sides of the balloon but only a little at the top and by the neck. The ones at the sides are under lots of tension and they rip apart if you pierce them. The ones at the ends still have plenty of stretch in them and will simply stretch around the skewer when you pierce the balloon.

Balloon Rocket

This balloon rocket is easy to make, but it really does go! Try making one in your backyard with a good long piece of kite string or fishing line, or you can do it indoors, but get an adult's permission first! This project is much easier with a friend to help you.

What you need

- About 16 ft (4.5 m) of kite string or fishing line—the smoother the string, the faster your rocket will go
- Drinking straw
- Balloon—the long torpedo-shaped ones are best
- Balloon pump
- Sticky tape

1

Choose two objects to tie the string to—for example, garden chairs, trees, or fences. They should be about 10–15 ft (3–5 m) apart, but they don't have to be at exactly the same height—your rocket can fly uphill or downhill. Tie one end of the string to one of the objects.

TRY THIS!

If you have enough space, try having a balloon rocket race with another line of string and a second balloon.

2

Thread the other end of the string through the drinking straw.

Inside the science

Stand on a skateboard and push against a wall—what happens?
You move backward! A very famous scientist called Sir Isaac Newton said that "for every action there is an equal and opposite reaction." In other words, you push on the wall and the wall pushes back.

In the balloon rocket experiment, the air has been forced into the stretchy balloon, which is trying to squeeze it out again. When you let go, the air is forced out very quickly—pushing one way—so the balloon moves the opposite way. This forward motion is called "thrust." In a real rocket, thrust is created by the force of burning rocket fuel in the rocket's engine— as the engines blast down, the rocket goes up!

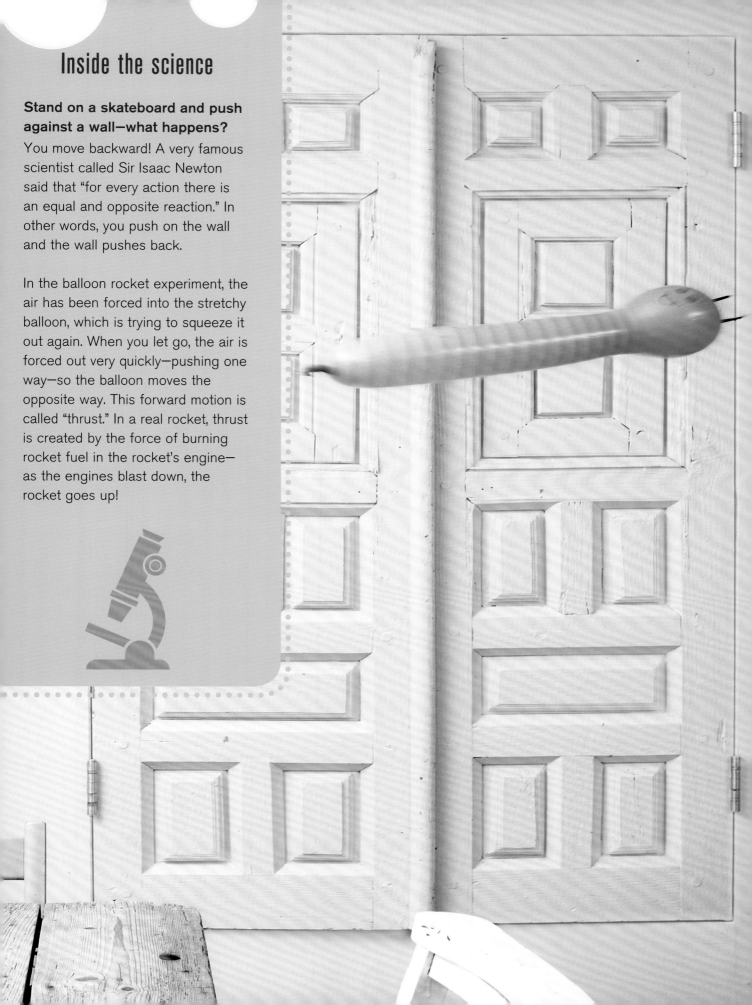

3

Now get your friend to help you pull the string as tight as possible while you tie it to the other object.

4

Inflate the balloon—using a balloon pump if you have one—but don't knot it. Twist the end and hold it closed while your friend tapes the straw to the balloon in two different places. The balloon opening will be the back of the rocket so make sure the front is facing along the string.

LET'S INVESTIGATE

You can launch your rocket over and over again and use a stopwatch to time the results. Try it with different shaped balloons—which shape goes fastest or furthest? Does the angle of the string make a difference? Does the length of the straw make a difference? Try it using a different type of twine or string.

5

To launch your rocket; simply let the end of the balloon go and see it shoot along the string!

Electric Balloon

Static electricity can make your hair stand on end when you take off a sweater. It can make sparks fly when you run along a carpeted corridor and then kiss someone. It sticks clothes together in a tumble drier, and it can also make balloons have strange powers. Find out about some of them.

What you need

- Balloons
- Balloon pump
- Twine, string, or yarn
- Empty aluminum soda can

1

Inflate two balloons and then rub each one on your hair for a little while. As you lift them away your hair will follow the balloon and stand on end. If it doesn't, rub a bit more.

2

Tie a string to each balloon. Hold one in each hand and bring them together. Can you make them touch?

LET'S INVESTIGATE

Inflate more balloons and try rubbing each one on different surfaces—carpet, a woolen sweater, a cotton sweatshirt, and a polyester shirt—before trying the can or water trick again. Which surface makes the can or water move most? If you put a few drops of water in the can to increase its weight will it still move? How much are you able to add before it is too heavy to move?

Inside the science

This experiment involves electricity! An object can be negatively charged, positively charged, or neutral (no charge). Objects with the same charge repel each other, which means push each other away (a bit like magnets do). Objects with different charges attract. If one object is charged and the other isn't, they also attract.

When you rub the balloon on your hair, negatively charged electrons jump from your hair to the balloon so the balloon is negatively charged—this is static electricity. Since the other balloon is also negatively charged, the two balloons will push away from each other. When an object has no charge, it means that positive and negative charges are cancelling each other out, so taking away negatively charged electrons from your hair leaves behind a positive charge. Since negative attracts positive, your hair is attracted to the balloon and stands on end. The same happens with the can and the water. Both of them are neutral so are attracted to the negatively charged balloon: The water bends and the can rolls.

3

Put a can on its side. Now hold a balloon near to, but not touching, the side of the can. Will the can follow the balloon when you move it slowly backward?

4

Rub the balloon on your hair again to build up some more static charge. Turn on a faucet (tap) until there is a small but steady trickle of cold water (not drops). Slowly move the balloon toward the water, but don't touch it. Did you see the water bend? If it didn't, try rubbing the balloon some more and have an even smaller stream of water.

Black and White Balloons

Have you ever been told that wearing white clothes will keep you cooler on a hot a day, or that if the ice caps melt the world will get warmer because ice reflects more heat than water? This dramatic balloon experiment, which you need to do on a sunny day, will make you believe it.

What you need

• Black balloon, white balloon, balloons in other colors (all the balloons should be the same shape and size)

• Balloon pump

• Twine or string

• Two pairs of safety goggles

• Magnifying glass

• Second timer

1 Choose a sunny day. Inflate the balloons until they are all a similar size and tie them off. Tie strings to them and then take them outside and tie them to a chair or railings so they don't blow away.

2 Both you and your helper should put on safety goggles. Take the white balloon. Hold the magnifying glass and focus the sun's rays onto the side of the white balloon. You need to move it backward and forward toward the balloon until you get a small dot of really intense light. Hold it there for 10 seconds (count out loud). Does anything happen to the balloon?

3

Now take the black balloon. Focus the sun onto it and begin timing. How far can you count before the balloon bursts? Keep going with the other balloons.

LET'S INVESTIGATE

Keep a record of how long it takes before the balloons burst. Which colors burst quickly? Which hold out for longer? Why?

Inside the science

We see when light bounces (reflects) off an object into our eyes. White light is a mixture of all the colors of the rainbow. When we see a white object, we are seeing all the colors mixed together reflecting off the object. When we see a colored object, we are seeing that color reflected while all the other colors are absorbed by it (go into it). When something is black, it means all the colors are absorbed and nothing is reflected. (A hole in a closed box looks black because all the light goes into the box and nothing comes out.)

When you focus the sunlight onto the white balloon, it is mostly reflected and the balloon doesn't heat up, the rubber doesn't melt, and the balloon doesn't burst. When you focus sunlight on the black balloon, most of the light is absorbed. The energy in the light causes the balloon to heat up and the rubber melts—bang! The other colored balloons will absorb some of the sunlight, so they may take a little longer to burst than the black one.

Balloon Fire Extinguisher

This is another experiment where balloons burst—you may need to get some help so you can cover your ears! Have you ever heard of the fire triangle? The fire triangle tells you that three things are needed for a fire to burn—fuel, heat, and oxygen. Take away any of those and the fire will go out. Find out which of three balloon fire extinguishers will put out a candle—the balloons will need to burst before they work!

What you need

- Balloon pump
- 3 similar-sized balloons in different colors, ideally white, blue, and yellow
- Teaspoon
- Baking soda (bicarbonate of soda)
- Small plastic bottle—the balloon neck must be able to fit over the top of the bottle
- Funnel
- Tablespoon
- Vinegar
- Water
- 2 sets of safety goggles
- Votive candle (tea light)
- Matches or lighter
- Second timer

1

Use the pump to inflate each of the balloons a few times so that they are well stretched, then let them deflate.

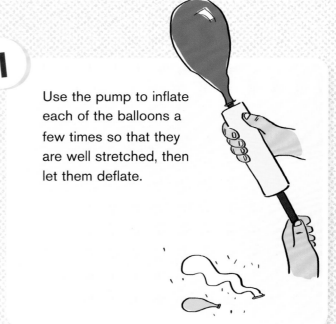

2

Put 3 teaspoons of baking soda (bicarbonate of soda) into the bottle. Use the funnel to pour about 2 tablespoons of vinegar into the yellow balloon.

3

Taking care not to spill the vinegar, stretch the neck of the yellow balloon over the top of the bottle.

4

Now hold the balloon up so that the vinegar spills into the bottle. The vinegar and baking soda (bicarbonate of soda) will react to produce a foam of carbon dioxide gas, which will inflate the balloon (see page 30). If it doesn't inflate that much, twist the neck of the balloon so no carbon dioxide escapes (you'll need a helper at this point), add some more baking soda and vinegar to the bottle, and then reattach the balloon. When it is well inflated, tie it off.

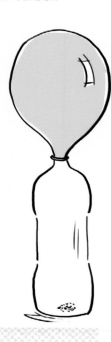

SAFETY FIRST

Always make sure candles are properly extinguished and don't place them near to flammable materials.

5

Now inflate the white balloon, using the pump, until it is about the same size as the yellow balloon and tie it off.

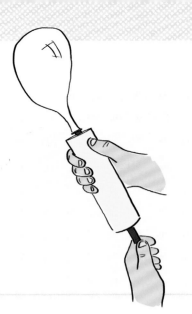

6

Wash out the funnel and use it to pour 4 or 5 tablespoons of water into the blue balloon. Now use the pump to inflate it until it is the same size as the white and yellow ones. You now have three balloon fire extinguishers—which do you think will put out a fire or, in this case, a candle?

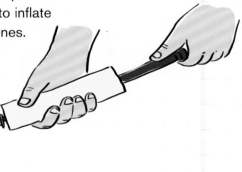

7

You will need an adult's help for the testing stage and you will both need to wear safety goggles. Ask an adult to light a votive candle (tea light). If you are feeling brave, hold the white, air-filled balloon just above the candle (NOT in the flame) for exactly 15 seconds or until the balloon bursts—whichever is quicker. What happens to the balloon and the flame?

8

Next, try with the blue, water-filled balloon. Hold it above the flame for exactly 15 seconds or until it bursts—whichever is quicker. What happens to the balloon and flame?

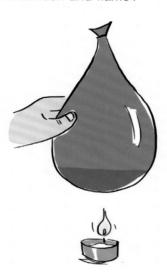

9

Finally, use the yellow carbon dioxide-filled balloon for exactly 15 seconds or until it bursts. What happens to the balloon and flame this time? Which was the best fire extinguisher?

LET'S INVESTIGATE

Check out what is in the fire extinguishers around your home and school. Look out for water and carbon dioxide, but you may also find foam and powder for different types of fires.

Inside the science

The sides of the fire triangle are fuel, heat, and oxygen. The fuel is the candle, which doesn't change for any balloon. The white balloon bursts because the heat of the candle melts the rubber, but it does not put out the flame because the air inside gives the candle more oxygen to burn. The blue balloon doesn't burst at all—the water takes away the heat from the candle (but not enough to put it out), so the rubber doesn't melt. If the rubber had melted, water would have put out the flame by taking heat away from it.

The yellow balloon bursts and extinguishes the flame because carbon dioxide gas is heavier than air. When the balloon bursts the gas sinks down over the flame and drives away all the oxygen.

Hovering Helium

What you need

- Store-bought helium balloon with a string or ribbon
- Lots of paper clips
- Sticky tack

Up until this experiment, the balloons we have used have been inflated with air or, in one case, with carbon dioxide. Air-filled balloons are great for playing games with because when you hit them up they come back down again. With helium balloons things are different; let one go outside, and it will fly into the air and disappear.

1

Once you are in the house, take any weights off the string of the balloon and let it go. Watch it sail up until it hits the ceiling.

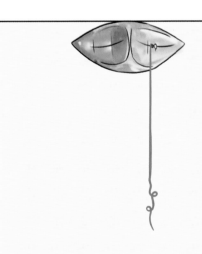

STAY SAFE

Don't take your foil balloon outside in case it floats away. Escaped foil balloons can be dangerous if they hit power lines and all balloons can harm wildlife when they eventually come back to earth.

2

Catch the string and slide on paper clips until the balloon sinks down and the string touches the floor.

LET'S INVESTIGATE

Let the balloon hang in space. How long will it float before it sinks to the floor? Get two helium balloons—an ordinary latex balloon and a shiny foil balloon. Get them both to hang in space. Which do you think will drop to the ground first? If you can get quite a lot of helium balloons, find out how many are needed to lift a favorite toy off the ground for a balloon ride.

3

Now take off one paper clip—does the balloon rise to the ceiling again or can you get it to hover so the balloon doesn't touch the ceiling and the string doesn't touch the floor? Use little balls of sticky tack attached to a paper clip to get it exactly right, hanging in space.

Inside the science

Helium gas is lighter than air so a balloon filled with helium gas weighs less than the air that would have filled the space taken up by the balloon. This means that the helium will float, just like a piece of wood will float on water. The difference is that the water has a surface—the water pushes the wood up until it floats on the surface. Air has no surface so the helium balloon will keep rising until the air thins out higher in the atmosphere and the weight of the helium equals the weight of the air it has displaced. The balloons deflate and sink after a while because there are tiny spaces between the molecules of the balloon through which the helium molecules can escape.

How Your Lungs Work

Usually we inflate a balloon by blowing air into it. In this experiment we suck the air into it, which is exactly how your lungs work.

What you need

- Plastic bottle
- Sharp scissors
- Two balloons
- Strong sticky tape (duct tape)
- Drinking straw
- Sticky tack
- Balloon pump
- Small elastic band

1

Carefully cut the bottom off the plastic bottle. Tie a knot in the neck of one of the balloons. Cut open the other end and then stretch the balloon across the open base of the bottle. It should be very tight. Secure it with strong sticky tape.

TOP TIP

Use a transparent plastic bottle for this experiment and remove the labels so that you have a clear view of the balloon lung!

2

Make a hole in the bottle top. You may need to ask an adult to help you with this—you can do it with pointy scissors, but using a hand drill is an easier way. The hole needs to be just big enough to push the straw through.

3

Cut a piece of straw about 4 in. (10 cm) long and push it half through the hole in the bottle top. Mold some sticky tack around the hole to make an airtight seal.

4

Inflate the second balloon and then let the air out again (to make it easy to inflate). Use an elastic band to attach the balloon to the straw below the lid. Twist the elastic over several times so that it is very tight.

Inside the science

Pulling the balloon down makes a bigger space inside the bottle for the same amount of air, which means the air pressure is lower. Air outside the bottle tries to get in to even out the pressure but it can only get into the balloon, so the balloon inflates. The same thing happens inside your chest.

Below your lungs you have a big muscle called the diaphragm, which is stretched across your chest. When it is relaxed it is a dome shape, but when you breathe in it flattens, pulling down just like the balloon. This makes a bigger space in your lungs. At the same time your ribs move up and out making an even bigger space. Air rushes into your lungs to even out the pressure, so you breathe in. Then the diaphragm relaxes and goes back to a dome shape, your ribs drop back, the pressure in the lungs increases, and the air rushes out—you breathe out.

LET'S INVESTIGATE

Try this experiment with different-sized bottles. Does the size of the bottle affect how much you can inflate the balloon?

5

Push the balloon attached to the bottle top into the bottle and screw on the lid.

6

Gently pull on the balloon at the base of the bottle and you should see the balloon inside the bottle inflate.

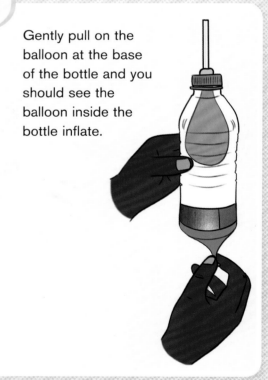

Weighing Air

What you need

- String or yarn
- Length of dowel or bamboo skewer about 12 in. (30 cm) long
- Two balloons
- Balloon pump
- Pin

Does air really weigh something? Lift your hand up—you can't feel any air pressing down on it. If you did the same in water. you would feel the weight of water. Here is a way of proving that air does weigh something.

1

Cut a piece of string about 12 in. (30 cm) long. Wrap one end tightly around the center of the dowel three or four times and tie a tight knot.

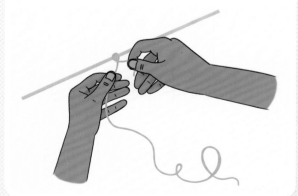

2

Tie the other end to the handle of a high kitchen cabinet so the dowel hangs freely below it. Push the string along the dowel (it should still be tight and difficult to move) until the dowel is balanced and horizontal.

3 Inflate the two balloons with a balloon pump until they are the same size and tie them off. Don't blow them up or you will be weighing the gas you breathe out, which isn't the same as air! Tie short lengths of string to each of them and then tie them tightly to the two ends of the dowel. Move the balloons along the dowel until they are balanced and the dowel is horizontal again. (Moving a balloon toward the center will make it appear to weigh less.)

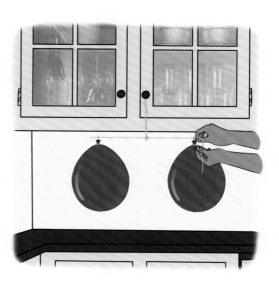

4

Use the pin to carefully pierce one balloon near the tied knot (see page 100). You don't want the balloon to burst suddenly but to let the air out slowly. If it is being very slow make a few more holes.

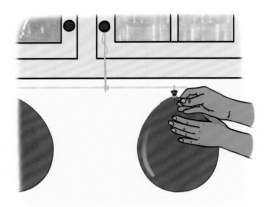

5

Watch as the balloon deflates. The burst balloon will rise up and the inflated balloon will drop, showing it is now heavier: Air has weight!

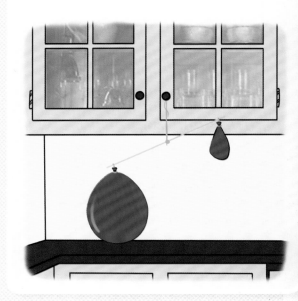

Inside the science

Air is made up of different invisible gases. Dry air is nearly 80 percent nitrogen and 20 percent oxygen, with tiny amounts of argon and carbon dioxide. Most air also contains water vapor—if the day is described as humid, it means there is a lot of water in the air. All this gas presses down on you. That pressure is called air pressure.

Imagine a square with sides of 1 in. (2.5 cm). A column of air on top of that square inch which reaches from sea level to the top of the Earth's atmosphere would have a weight of about 14.7 lb (6.67 kg). (If you go up a mountain, there is less air above you so the air pressure is less.) That weight is pressing down on you all the time from all directions but since you have never known any different you don't feel it. This experiment proves it weighs something!

LET'S INVESTIGATE

Try the experiment with two identical zip lock bags—one flat and one blown up with air. They will weigh the same. The balloon experiment works because a lot of air is forced into the stretchy balloon under high pressure. This air is denser (has more molecules in it) than in the surrounding air.

Explore Further

There are some fantastic science websites and videos online.
Here are just a few that might interest you:

Ducksters Education Site

http://www.ducksters.com/science/

This website explains many of the complicated ideas of science, including atoms and electrons.

Exploratorium

https://www.exploratorium.edu/explore

The San Francisco Exploratorium is a great place to visit, and the online activities are worth exploring too.

Popular Science

https://www.popsci.com/science-behind-popping-balloon

Watch this slow-motion video of a popping balloon.

Science Kids

http://www.sciencekids.co.nz/

A fun website with scientific facts, experiments, games, and quizzes.

Science Made Simple

http://www.sciencemadesimple.com/projects.html

A website that starts with interesting questions and gives answers, and there are projects to try out.

The Science Explorer

http://www.exploratorium.edu/science_explorer/

This website has lots of great experiments to try.

YouTube

Absolute Genius with Dick and Dom
https://www.youtube.com/channel/UCWYbThn3fIVZCueobkjq1yQ

A series that explores the work of the most important inventors and scientists in history. The ideas are explained with lots of whacky experiments.

Sick Science
https://www.youtube.com/user/Stevespanglerscience

A series of awesome science demonstrations.

Slow-motion Bubble Bursting
https://www.youtube.com/watch?v=ktvZ2Z_s4Bo

Watch this slow-motion video of a bubble bursting!

Index

air pressure 23
allergies 104
anus 67
appendix 67
arms
    bones 39
    muscles 52–53, 56
arteries 67, 68, 82, 88, 89
asthma 96
astronauts 40
atrium 82, 83
auditory canal 18
axon 116, 117, 118

bacteria 66, 77
    immune system 101, 104–5
    in intestines 75, 77
    on skin 30
    on teeth 72
balance 18, 21–22, 54, 55, 108
bicep 52–53, 56
bladder 67, 98
blind spot 16
blinking 12, 13, 114
blood 82–87
    cells 66, 83, 84, 86, 88, 104
    circulation 82–83, 88–89, 94
    made in bones 38
    nutrients 77, 86
    waste products 98–100
bones
    broken 44–47
    ear 19
    exercise 54
    function 38
    growing 54
    in hand 39, 59–60
    joints 43
    skeleton 38–39
    vitamins/minerals 42
brain 66, 107–9
    cerebral cortex hat 110–13
    confusing 124–25
    connections 119–21
    dreams 108, 126
    memory 108, 113, 122–23
    nervous system 116–21
    reaction times 114–15, 118
    stem 108, 109, 114
breathing 80, 92, 94, 96, 97, 108

calcium 42, 68
canine teeth 70
carbon dioxide 72, 86, 88, 94
carpals 39, 59
cells 66, 116, 117, 118
cerebellum/cerebrum 108, 109
circulation 82–83, 88
clavicle 39
coccyx 39, 48
cochlea 18, 20
constipation 75
cooling down 35
cornea 10, 12
cuts 87, 101

dendrites 116, 118
dentin 68
dermis 28
diaphragm 67, 96
digestive system 66–79, 108
    gut string model 78–81
    poop 74–77
    teeth 68–71
disease 104, 105
dreams 108, 126–27
drinking water 75, 98

ear drum 18, 20, 21
ears 18–23, 101, 113
enamel 68
epidermis 28
epiglottis 24, 80
esophagus 24, 67, 76, 78
Eustachian tube 18, 23, 24
excretory system 98–100
exercise 35, 54–55, 91, 92, 108,
    115
eyebrow 11, 34
eyelashes 12
eyelids 12, 30
eyes 10–17
    and balance 22
    brain role 113, 114, 115, 124–25
    colour 13
    eye socket 39
    testing 16–17

face 11, 53, 58
feet 30, 39
femur 39

fiber 75
fibula 39
fingers 30, 39, 59
first aid 80, 87, 101
fitness 54–55
flexibility 50–51, 55
food
    containing iron 87
    digestive system 66, 75
    taste and smell 24–27, 113
fungi 101

gallbladder 67
goosebumps 33, 108

hair 28, 33–34, 101
hands 59–63
    bones 39, 59
    nerves 30
    robot hand 60–63
    washing 101
hearing 18–20, 21, 113
heart 66, 67, 82–83
    how it works 90–93, 108
    valves 82, 83, 88–89, 90
hormones 86, 108
humerus 39
hypothalamus 108, 109

immune system 66, 101–5
incisors 70
incus 18
infections 86, 101, 103, 104
inner ear 18
intestines 67, 76–77, 80–81
iris 10, 12
iron 87

jaw muscle 58
joints 43, 54

kidneys 66, 67, 98, 99–100
Kim's game 122–23

larynx 20, 24
legs 30, 39, 58, 114
lens 10
ligaments 43
liver 66, 67, 77
lungs 66, 67, 83, 89, 94–97, 108

malleus 18
memory 108, 113, 122–23
metacarpals 39, 59
metatarsals 39
middle ear 18, 20, 23
molars 70, 75
mucous 101, 102
muscles 38, 52–58
    arm 52–53, 56
    brain role 108, 116
    exercising 54–55
    hand 60, 63
    heart 92
    model 56–58
    skeletal 52
    smooth 77
myelin sheath 116, 118

nasal cavity 24
neck vertebrae 39
nerves
    optic 10, 16, 109, 115
    in skin 28, 29, 30, 31, 32
    spinal cord 48, 114, 115, 116
    in teeth 68
nervous system 116–27
neurons 66, 116–21
nose
    smell 24, 25–26, 27
    snot 101, 102–3

oesophagus 24, 67, 76, 78
optic nerve 10, 16, 109, 115
oral cavity 24
organs 38, 66–67
outer ear 18
oxygen 83, 88, 89, 94

pancreas 67, 77
patella 39
pathogens 101, 104
pelvis 38, 39
phalanges 39, 59
pinhole camera 14–15
pinna 18, 24
pituitary gland 108, 109
plaque 72–73
plasma 83, 86, 88
platelet 83, 87
poop 74–77

pre-molars 70
projects, difficulty 7
pulp 68
pupil 10, 12, 13, 114

radius 39, 59
reaction times 118
rectum 67
reflexes 114
retina 10, 16, 115
rib cage 38, 39, 96
road, crossing 17

saliva 75, 101
scapula 39
sebaceous gland 28
semicircular canals 18, 21, 22
senses
    brain role 108, 113, 116
    ears 18–23
    eyes 10–17
    smell 24, 25–26
    taste 26–27, 113
    touch 29–32, 113
sign language 59

singing 20
skeleton 38–49
skin 28–32
    body hair 28, 33–34
    cooling down 35
    immune system 101
    sunburn 35
    washing 35, 101
skull 38, 39, 110
sleep 127
sling, making 46–47
smell 24, 25–26, 27
snot 101, 102–3
sound 18–20, 21, 113
speech 20, 108, 110t
spinal cord 48, 108, 109, 114,
    115, 116
spine 38, 39, 48–51
spleen 67
sport 54–55, 92, 96, 108, 115
stapes 18
sternum 39
stethoscope 90–91
stomach 67, 76, 78
strength 54, 55, 92

subcutaneous tissue 28
sugar 26
sunburn 35
sunglasses 13
sweating 28, 35, 108
synaptic terminal 116, 118

tarsals 39
taste 26, 27, 113
tears 12, 101
teeth 24, 39, 68–71
    jaw muscle 58
    plaque 72–73
    and sugar 26
    vitamins/minerals 42
temperature
    of body 87, 108
    skin 31–32, 33
tendons 52, 63
thumb 63
tibia 39
tongue 24, 26
touch 29–32, 113
trachea 67, 80
triceps 52–53, 56

ulna 39, 59
ureter 67
urethra 67, 98
urine 98

vaccinations 104, 105
valve, heart 82, 83, 88–89, 90
veins 67, 82, 88, 89
ventricle 82, 83, 109
vertebrae 39, 48
viruses 101, 104–5
Vitamin D 35, 42
voice box 20, 24

washing 35, 101
wee 98
windpipe (trachea) 67, 80

Acknowledgment

Many thanks to my nephew, Robert Carter, for making sure that, although the science stayed simple, it was still correct.

Picture Credits

All photography by Terry Benson, except for:

Getty Images/
Adam Gault p. 73, Andrew Mitchell/Eye Em p. 62, Astra Astrid Indricane/Eye Em p. 114, Chayse Sly/Eye Em p. 29, Chris Stein p. 19, Dave King p. 89, Debby Lewis-Harrison p. 75, Education Images p. 119, Elaine Booth/Eye Em p. 21, Elisabeth Schmitt p. 87, Elva Etienne p. 17, Henrik Sorensen p. 39, JGI/Jamie Grill p. 123, JGI/Tom Grill p. 10, ONOKY—Eric Audras p. 86, Peter Muller p. 27, Robert Kneschke/Eye Em p. 90, Taweesak Baongern/Eye Em p. 116, Tetra Images p. 101